Secrets of

ENERGY
WORK

Secrets of

ENERGY WORK

PAUL BRECHER

A Dorling Kindersley Book

Dorling **DK** Kindersley

LONDON, NEW YORK, SYDNEY, DELHI, PARIS,
MUNICH and JOHANNESBURG

To my second son, Zak, who is first equal in my heart.

This book was conceived, designed and produced by
THE IVY PRESS LIMITED,
The Old Candlemakers, Lewes, East Sussex BN7 2NZ

Art director *Peter Bridgewater*
Editorial director *Sophie Collins*
Designer *Kevin Knight, Jane Lanaway*
Editor *Rowan Davies*
Picture researchers *Liz Eddison, Vanessa Fletcher*
Photography *Guy Ryecart*
Illustrations *Sarah Young, Catherine McIntyre,
Michael Courtney, Andrew Milne, Ivan Hissey*
Calligraphy *Linsey Tai*

First published in Great Britain in 2001 by
DORLING KINDERSLEY LIMITED,
9 Henrietta Street, London WC2E 8PS

A CIP catalogue record for this book is
available from the British Library

ISBN 0 7513 1200 2

Originated and printed by
Hong Kong Graphic and Printing Limited, China

see our complete
catalogue at
www.dk.com

CONTENTS

Balance
The ancient Chinese concepts of yin and yang are central to the ideas in this book.

HOW TO USE THIS BOOK

To make *The Secrets of Energy Work* simple to use, it is divided into sections giving either information or practical instructions. In addition, concise background information about the chi kung exercises is followed by easy-to-follow step-by-step guides illustrated with colour photographs. It is best to work through the exercises in the sequence in which they appear, rather than selecting exercises at random. This is because the practice of chi kung initially focuses on physical health, but as training progresses it becomes more abstract, focusing on the mind, emotions and spirit – and this is reflected in the sequence of exercises.

Important Notice
If you have a high grade fever, a severe infection or an inflammatory condition then you should seek medical treatment before practising these exercises. People suffering from severe neuro-biological or psychiatric disorders should not practise these techniques. This book is for reference purposes only, and ideally the exercises within it should be carried out under the supervision of a trained teacher.

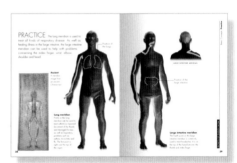

Basic concepts
This section provides background information and may be referred to when you are doing the exercises.

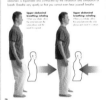

Theory
These spreads explain the exercise – what it is and how to gain optimum benefit.

Practice
These spreads show you how to perform the exercise with step-by-step photographs.

The spirit body
The final section of the book shows you how to practice spiritual exercise at the highest level.

Energy in the Body

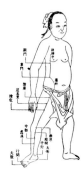

Invisible channels
Meridians are energy channels in the body used in Chinese acupuncture.

Every culture in the history of the world has, in one way or another, acknowledged the existence of a life-force energy in the human body. The Indians call it *prana*, the Chinese call it *chi*, and the Japanese call it *ki*. In the West it is called human electricity.

This energy can be attained and expressed in different ways, and so again each culture interprets it slightly differently. For example, *prana* and *chi*, as well as meaning

"energy", also mean "breath", because one can generate energy by practising special breathing exercises.

In Chinese and Japanese culture, a painting of a landscape is considered to be a great work of art if the artist's energy was in tune with the land as he painted it, and if he was able to express this unity by using the energy to create a harmonious painting.

In the West, athletes in training are required to consume vast amounts of high-calorie food so that they have enough strength to achieve their physical goals: a calorie is a scientific term that describes a unit of energy.

In addition, thought processes can be measured electronically. Mental states emit types of energy known as alpha, beta, or gamma brain waves.

By practising the chi kung exercises in this book on a regular basis, you will be able to increase your energy and encourage its smooth flow around the body, promoting good physical health and longevity, with greater mental power and spiritual development.

Discovering acupuncture

In September 1991, Erika and Helmut Simon were walking in the Otztal Alps on the border between Austria and Italy, when they found a body that had been revealed by the melting glacial ice. Carbon-dating tests revealed the body to be that of a middle-aged man who had frozen to death 5,300 years before. The body was tattooed with acupuncture meridians and points. The man had probably been tattooed by an acupuncturist to enable him to treat himself, or they were intended for use by another acupuncturist at a later date.

The points that were chosen to treat the man's problems show a certain level of sophistication, revealing that the acupuncturist who performed the treatment had a deep knowledge of acupuncture, implying that it must have been developed at a much earlier period. So we learn that acupuncture was a fully developed medical system in central Europe at the same time that it was used in ancient China – at least 5,500 years ago.

WORLDWIDE LIFE-FORCE

In both East and West, human energy is seen as an animating force within us that keeps us alive and enables us to reach not only physical goals and good health, but also artistic and creative achievements. Here are some examples, from around the world, of attitudes to the human life-force that are testament not only to the universality of the understanding of human energy, but also to its antiquity.

Alaska

Alaska
The Aleutian Islanders have their own acupuncture system. Their medical terminology is unique to their indigenous language and has no link to the Chinese words for the same anatomical aspects.

The world
Every known culture in the history of the world has described the existence of a life-force energy within the human body.

China

Acupuncture was in use at least 5,500 years ago in ancient China, where it was a fully developed medical system.

India

In India the life-force is known as prana, literally "the breath of life".

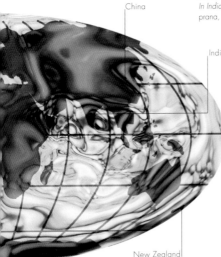

China

India

New Zealand

New Zealand

The Maoris used to carve lines into their flesh to express the idea of the energy flowing through their bodies, a practice later replaced by tattooing.

The Chinese Perspective

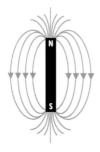

Polarity
Like a magnet, our internal energy has both a positive and a negative flow.

Although the existence of an energy system in the body is common to many cultures, in this book the Chinese perspective will be stressed because in the West we are more familiar with it. Chinese acupuncture is now so accepted that it is offered by doctors on the National Health Service in the United Kingdom, and is recommended and promoted by the World Health Organization (WHO). The WHO hopes that its practice will spread internationally, because it is low in cost and effective.

Traditional Chinese medicine refers to the invisible energy pathways in the body as meridians. There are various areas on those meridians that can influence the energy flow within them. These are called acupuncture or meridian points. The animating life-force energy of the body, which gives us the power to walk, talk and think, is called *chi*. In Chinese medicine, the flow of chi is extremely important for maintaining health.

In Western medicine, homeostasis is the process by which opposing forces in the body try to maintain a balanced state as external environmental factors change. Chinese medicine interprets this as maintaining the balance of yin and yang. *Yin* and *yang* are terms used to describe forces at work in the world, and can be applied to all things, including the body. They are interacting, interdependent opposites. For example, high and low blood pressure, or oedema and dehydration, are conditions in which the yin–yang of the body is out of balance.

Magnetic poles

If we combine the ideas of chi and yin
and yang, we can say that our internal
energy has both a positive and a
negative flow. A magnet has positive
and negative poles, and it is the same
with the body – we have yin negative
meridians and yang positive meridians.
When yin and yang are in perfect
balance and our chi is flowing evenly
and smoothly, with no obstructions, we
are in a state of neutrality – warm and
calm and at ease with ourselves and
the world. When we are in this state
of good health, physically, mentally,
emotionally, and spiritually, it is called
wu chi. This state is not a one-off
spiritual high – it is a way of being that
we try to maintain in our everyday lives.
When yin and yang are out of
balance, health problems may arise.
The exercises in this book will enable
you to enter into a state of wu chi.
However, the ability to remain healthy,
calm, and steady through our everyday
stressful lives comes with many years of
training; in fact, I am still training.

Yellow Emperor 2697–2597BC
The Yellow Emperor's Classic on Internal
Medicine provided the foundation of
acupuncture and chi kung energy work.

CHI KUNG ORIGINS Chi kung
energy work has been practised in China for thousands of
years and is mentioned in many ancient Chinese books. There are two main
texts worth drawing attention to, because they are so influential and of such
great antiquity. The first is the *Yi Jing*, known in the West as *The I Ching Book
of Changes*. The second is called *The Yellow Emperor's Classic on Internal
Medicine* (*Huang Di Nei Jing*); it provides the basis of chi kung energy work.

I CHING

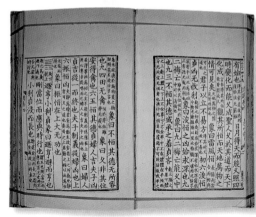

**The I Ching
Book of Changes**
*Written by Fu Xi
in 2852BC, the
I Ching reveals the
workings of chi.*

Chinese medicine

In traditional Chinese medicine, doctors use the pulse on the wrist to diagnose any imbalance of chi in the meridians.

Monks

Buddhist and Taoist monks preserve many ancient chi kung techniques to the present day.

The Origins of Chi Kung

Old master
*Chang San Feng (b.1247)
created the first tai chi style.*

The I Ching Book of Changes (Yi Jing) is one of the most important books in chi kung's history. It was written in 2852BC by Fu Xi, and was further classified and organized by Wen Wang, the first ruler of the state of Zhou, in 1122BC.

Wen Wang said that Fu Xi had been able to formulate the *Yi Jing* because he had spent a lifetime observing the energetic interaction of the sun, moon, and stars with all the various forms that nature took here on earth. He had studied the behaviour of animals and people, the fluctuations in the weather, and the variations in the seasons. Patterns had been discerned and expressed as variations in the relationship of the forces of yin and yang energy, chi.

The *Huang Di Nei Jing*, or *The Yellow Emperor's Classic on Internal Medicine*, was written by the Yellow Emperor (2697–2597BC). The fact that he lived to such a great age was attributed to his knowledge of how chi animates the body.

The book contains the philosophy and practical techniques that are the foundation of acupuncture and chi kung, and is the accumulated knowledge of many generations. It states that good health depends on chi flowing smoothly throughout the body, which is what all chi kung techniques are designed to achieve. Chi kung energy work is an ancient system, tried and tested over thousands of years.

The tai chi connection

One of the greatest martial artists and chi kung practitioners in the history of China was Chang San Feng, who was born in 1247. He put his knowledge of chi kung into his practice of martial arts in order to improve his health while training.

He eventually concentrated the essential principles into 12 movement sequences, which were called The 12 Chi Disruption Forms and were acknowledged as the first great tai chi system. Chang San Feng lived in the Wu Dang mountain range, and so his system is also known as Wu Dang Mountain Tai Chi.

During the nineteenth century this system was studied by Yang Lu Chan (1799–1872), who used it to invent his own style of exercises, which became known as The Old Yang Style of Tai Chi.

The chi kung exercises that feature throughout this book are taken from both The Old Yang Style and The 12 Chi Disruption Forms.

BASIC CONCEPTS

Before you start training in chi kung, it is advisable to get to grips with the basic ideas on which it is based. In this chapter, therefore, is a detailed explanation of the terminology you will encounter, such as chi, yin and yang, wu chi, meridians, and energy centres. ↭ Common questions are also dealt with here, such as who should practise chi kung, how long training sessions should last and what you should wear. In addition, because for most Westerners chi kung offers a completely new experience, there is a thorough explanation of what to expect once you start training, both physically and mentally. ↭ The section is rounded off with an in-depth look at meridians, which are vital to an understanding of the practice of chi kung.

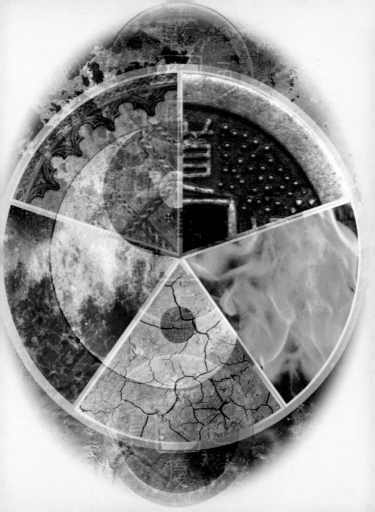

Chi, Yin and Yang, and Wu Chi

Chi is an easy term to comprehend if it is thought of as a type of electromagnetic force. The electric charges that are involved are very small, just like when two people touch and experience a spark of static electricity. In the same way that electricity enables a radio to produce sound, a television to produce images, and a bulb to produce light, chi enables us to move, see, and speak.

Everything people do is because of their chi; the more chi we have, the more active and creative we can be and the more we can achieve. The whole world is interconnected by chi – every creature, person, and plant is part of the web of life whose strands are made of chi. Chi kung exercises heal the body by encouraging chi to flow through the acupuncture meridians.

Progression
When yin and yang are balanced we can return to the state of wu chi.

This feels rather like glowing, warm, electrically charged water circulating through the body.

The terms yin and yang simply refer to interacting opposites anywhere in the universe. The balancing of yin and yang chi in the body is the basis of energy work and the key to good health on all levels, not just the physical. In a health context, a yin condition means chi deficiency – this needs to be replenished. A yang condition denotes an excess of chi that needs to be reduced.

Once yin and yang have been balanced, it is then easier to enter into a state of wu chi. The state of wu chi is a spiritual dimension in which you become aware that not only are you interconnected to the world, but that it is within you as much as you are within it.

Unifying principle

Wu chi is attainable through everyday activities, not just through chi kung. When it happens, it is different for each person, but in all cases there is an element of unity. Some people, when walking in a forest, feel at one with nature; others, in a moment of deep love, feel unified with their partner. What makes chi kung special is that it is a way of getting to wu chi intentionally, rather than occasionally and accidentally stumbling upon it.

This book enables individuals to harmonize their internal world – mind and emotions, body and spirit. Then, when people are balanced within themselves, they can achieve harmony in their relationships with others and the world around them.

More Information

For more information on **spiritual development** see page 206.

MERIDIANS AND ENERGY CENTRES

The acupuncture meridians run throughout the body, connecting every part of it together. There are 12 major meridians, named after the internal organs they are connected to. The internal organs are like reservoirs of the body's energy, and the meridians are like rivers that flow from them. These 12 meridians pass through the internal organs to the tips of the toes, top of the head, and ends of the fingers. The meridians carry energy to and from the body's energy centres: the three tan tien and the seven chakras.

Meridians
The World Health Organization published a report in 1991 detailing over 400 acupuncture points and the 20 meridians as part of their policy to promote acupuncture worldwide.

Tan tien
The body contains an energy centre in the abdomen known as the "tan tien", literally "field of the elixir of life".

Chakras

*The chakras are energy centres
located on the thrusting meridian,
which rises up the centre of the body.*

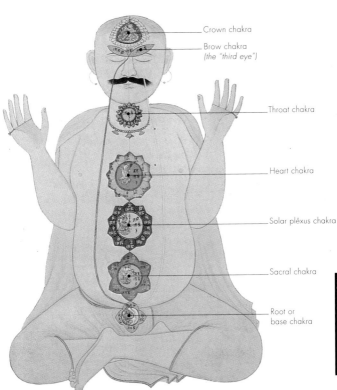

Crown chakra

Brow chakra
(the "third eye")

Throat chakra

Heart chakra

Solar plexus chakra

Sacral chakra

Root or
base chakra

The 12 Organs

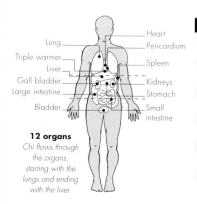

Lung
Triple warmer
Liver
Gall bladder
Large intestine
Bladder

Heart
Pericardium
Spleen
Kidneys
Stomach
Small intestine

12 organs
Chi flows through the organs, starting with the lungs and ending with the liver.

THE CHI PEAKS	
Lung meridian	3 a.m.–5 a.m.
Large intestine meridian	5 a.m.–7 a.m.
Stomach meridian	7 a.m.–9 a.m.
Spleen meridian	9 a.m.–11 a.m.
Heart meridian	11 a.m.–1 p.m.
Small intestine meridian	1 p.m.–3 p.m.
Bladder meridian	3 p.m.–5 p.m.
Kidney meridian	5 p.m.–7 p.m.
Pericardium meridian	9 p.m.–11 p.m.
Triple warmer meridian	7 p.m.–9 p.m.
Gall bladder meridian	11 p.m.–1 a.m.
Liver meridian	1 a.m.–3 a.m.

Each of the 12 main meridians has a strong influence over one organ, from which it gets its name. The lungs are traditionally the start of the meridian system and are known as the chi storehouse. The flow of chi peaks in each meridian at different times of day.

The organs are categorized as being hollow or full. The lungs, kidneys, spleen, liver, heart, and pericardium are full organs. They all make and store substances: the lungs generate and store chi; the kidneys create and store essence (the vital force governing growth, reproduction and development); the spleen makes blood; the liver filters and stores blood; the heart pumps blood; and the pericardium protects (stores) the heart.

The stomach, small and large intestines, bladder, triple warmer, and gall bladder are hollow organs. They process food so it can be used by the body: the stomach receives food; the small and large intestines transmit and excrete waste; the bladder releases urine; the triple warmer releases heat; and the gall bladder releases bile.

Location of the organs

The organs are located in one of three body cavities. The upper body cavity is the area above the solar plexus: it contains the lungs, heart, pericardium, and brain. The middle cavity is the area between the solar plexus and the navel: it is where the spleen, pancreas, stomach, liver, and gall bladder are situated. The lower cavity is situated below the navel: it contains the large and small intestines, the kidneys, uterus and bladder.

Each organ is also linked with one of the five elements of wood, metal, earth, fire and water (a system used by the Chinese to describe natural energies). The lungs and large intestine are metal; the stomach and spleen are earth; the heart, small intestine, pericardium, and triple warmer are fire; the bladder and kidneys are water; and the gall bladder and liver are wood.

More Information

For more information on **meridian connections** see page 27.

Nature's way
The chi flow in the body changes in accordance with the seasons.

THE FIVE ELEMENTS In traditional

Chinese medicine, the mind, emotions, senses, internal organs, tissues and meridians are all interconnected. All aspects of life are based in the five elements: wood, fire, earth, metal and water. Each element controls organs and body functions, and is associated with a flavour, colour, and other aspects. For example, a person who has a weak spleen will feel anxious and crave sweet-tasting food; a person who consumes too much alcohol and suffers liver damage may have impaired vision; and old people with weak kidneys will feel the cold more in winter and their bones may ache.

Elemental power
The ancient Chinese were aware of the five elements and lived their lives in accordance with them.

Associations of the Five Elements

Element	Wood	Fire	Earth	Metal	Water
Organ	Liver Gall bladder	Heart Small intestine	Spleen Stomach	Lungs Large intestine	Kidneys Bladder
Yang Emotion	Anger	Hate, impatience	Worry, anxiety	Sadness, depression	Fear
Yin Emotion	Kindness	Love, joy, respect	Fairness, openness	Uprightness, courage	Gentleness
Expression	Shouting	Laughing	Singing	Weeping	Groaning
Season	Spring	Summer	Late summer	Autumn	Winter
Weather	Wind	Heat	Dampness	Dryness	Cold
Colour	Green	Red	Yellow	White	Black
Cycle	Growing	Fruitful	Ripe harvest	Seed falling	Sleeping
Time	Infancy	Youth	Adulthood	Old age	Death
Sense	Eyes	Tongue	Lips, mouth	Nose	Ears
Taste	Sour	Bitter	Sweet	Pungent	Salty
Nourishes	Nails, tendons, nerves	Blood, vessels	Muscles	Skin, hair	Bones, teeth, pubic hair

Before You Start

Morning glory
*The timing of chi kung training
is important: sunrise is best.*

Here are the answers to a few questions that are frequently asked by those considering beginning a chi kung programme. For further information, see the addresses section at the end of the book.

Who should practise chi kung?

Almost everybody can benefit from the practice of chi kung energy work. Weak and ill people can become stronger, and healthy people can reinforce their immune systems to reduce their chances of becoming ill. However, people with severe mental imbalance and those with acute problems such as a high-grade fever, inflammatory conditions or infections, should train only if they are supervised by a qualified chi kung teacher. They should also be receiving medical treatment. This book is for reference only and cannot take the place of correct instruction from a competent teacher.

Where and when should I train?

Although the chi kung energy work that we are discussing can be practised anywhere and at any time, the ideal situation is barefoot on grass, under or near a tree, at sunrise.

If you can, practise in a garden or park, or even better in some natural unspoilt woodland. In these places you are surrounded by nature, and can benefit from good oxygenated air, and the natural energy of the earth and plants. If it is damp, raining, cold, or windy, practise indoors. If inside, avoid draughts, and train in a warm, dry room with recently freshened air.

Sunrise is the best time for chi kung because the natural energy of the environment has not yet been disturbed by human activity. You will also be activating the body's chi at the optimum time for the lung meridian.

How long should I train?

The period spent training each day will vary, depending on your health and enthusiasm. Beginners should practise for at least 15 minutes each morning and evening. Intermediate level students can increase this to about 30 minutes twice daily. People at an advanced level, who have been training for a number of years and are aware of their strengths and weaknesses, can train for as long as desired.

Before and after

Begin a session by imagining you are protected by a cocoon of golden healing light. Afterwards, gather and store the chi in the lower tan tien.

More Information

For more information on **storing chi in the lower tan tien** see pages 88–95.

Footwear
If you have to wear shoes because the weather is cold or wet, boating shoes offer a sturdier option than Chinese slippers.

WHAT SHOULD YOU WEAR?

There is no special type of clothing needed to practise chi kung. Just make sure your clothes do not constrict your movement or blood flow. Therefore, it is especially important not to wear a very tight belt or a wristwatch. If you are practising outside and it is a bit cold, wear warm clothes to avoid catching a chill. If it is very sunny and hot, wear a hat to avoid getting heatstroke, or train in the shade. It is best to practise barefoot on grass, so that you can draw up energy from the earth through your feet, but wearing flat-soled shoes is also an option.

Calm
The tranquillity of water can help to calm the mind if you practise chi kung outdoors.

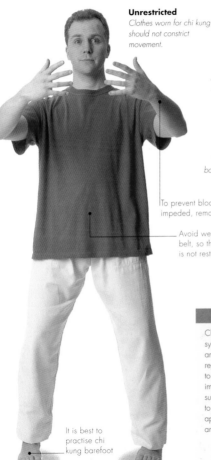

Unrestricted
Clothes worn for chi kung should not constrict movement.

Moderation
The rays of the sun can heal the body, but too much sun can overheat the body, heart and blood.

To prevent blood flow being impeded, remove your watch

Avoid wearing a tight belt, so that blood flow is not restricted

Self-Healing

Chi kung is a self-healing system that calms the mind and emotions. It also regulates the meridian chi to help heal the body. It is important to practise in a suitable environment and to dress in a way that is appropriate for the exercises and weather conditions.

It is best to practise chi kung barefoot

What to Expect

Axon (nerve fibre)

Nerve ending

Neuron cell body

Myelin sheath

Dendrites (nerve branches)

Neural pathway
Neurons, the cells in the nervous system, aid the flow of chi in the form of electricity as it flows through the body.

People who practise chi kung will experience chi energy flowing around their bodies through the meridians. This flow of energy invigorates blood circulation and warms the whole body. Therefore people with poor circulation or stiff joints benefit immensely from the practice of chi kung. It also helps improve many other health problems.

When chi flows freely, it feels like a warm, electrically charged glow. On the other hand, where chi flow is blocked or stagnant, there is a tendency for aches or pains to occur. This usually occurs in areas where there is a build-up of physical tension resulting from daily mental stress, or at the sites of particular health problems or old injuries.

Shaking

When chi is trying to break through a blocked area, mild shaking occurs. When the body (and especially the legs) start to shake very violently, this indicates complete exhaustion. If this happens to you, stop training, eat a large hot meal and take a rest. The third type of shaking is a humming vibration in the body, which feels like the sound of a bumble bee and is very beneficial. It happens when the chi is flowing smoothly through all the meridians and a person is in good health.

Tingling

Healing chi flowing around the body creates a feeling of calm and peaceful well-being. Students may also feel a tingling and fullness in their fingertips and other parts of the body. When a meridian is activated, you will feel its line of force through the body.

As your experience and practice of chi kung grows, chi begins to flow through the meridians more strongly, until you feel that your body is made entirely of energy.

Spiritual experiences

When you have a few years' experience, the practice of chi kung makes you feel as if an electromagnetic force-field is building up around the hands and body. You also have a sense of weightlessness, as if in zero gravity or moving through water.

At the highest level of chi kung, there are spiritual experiences beyond the physical. You acquire the sensation of expanding until you feel outside yourself, part of everything else, and at one with the world. You feel simultaneously that you are sinking into the earth and flying in the sky.

More Information

For more information on **spiritual flying** see page 212.

WHAT TO EXPECT

The strange thing about chi kung is that, to begin with, we exercise our body in order to activate energy. However, after years of practice, energy flows strongly, and the posture, movement, and breathing of chi kung become involuntary. It is a strange and enjoyable experience to find that chi is mobilizing you. At this stage we can appreciate the meditative qualities of chi kung – at first the mind had to be active in order to perform the exercises, but now it is no longer needed and you are free of it. This is true meditation.

Activating energy

When we practise any type of chi kung we have to hold the arms up and away from the body. The reason for this is to keep all the joints open, not folded up, so that chi can flow unimpeded along the meridians. However, after many years of accumulating energy within the body, we find that when we do our chi kung the energy expands through the body so strongly that it forces our arms up and out in front of us.

A radiant cocoon of
positive energy protects
the chi kung student

Arms should be
positioned up and
away from the body

Healing chi
*When chi flows around
the body it creates
a pleasant sensation
of calm well-being.*

Meridians and Organs: 1

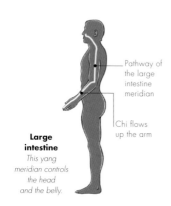

Pathway of the large intestine meridian

Chi flows up the arm

Large intestine
This yang meridian controls the head and the belly.

Meridians are classed as yin or yang, depending on whether they are situated on exposed or protected parts of the body. The yang channels are on the outer side of the limbs, while the yin channels are on the inner side. The meridians on the back of the torso are yang, while those on the front are yin. The yang meridians on the outer sides of the limbs are involved with resistance to disease and other adverse external factors. The yin meridians on the inner sides are more concerned with nourishing the body.

There are 8 secondary meridians that connect the 12 main organ meridians and regulate the chi in them. These meridians can be used to store excess energy that is generated through chi kung. Each of the 12 meridians influences a particular organ in the body. Each organ in turn controls other parts of the physical and emotional self. We shall look at each meridian in turn.

The lungs

If the chi in the lung meridian is strong, the body can resist exogenous pathogenic attack. Through intake of air, the lungs are the first major internal organs to come into contact with the environment. They must be kept strong through chi kung breathing so they can adapt to seasonal conditions – people succumb to attack by bacteria and viruses if the weather changes suddenly.

The skin is known as the third lung – if a person is painted all over, even if his mouth and nose are not obstructed, he will still die from suffocation. The skin is the body's first line of defence against invading micro-organisms. The pores of the skin open in hot weather to release heat, and close in cold weather to keep heat in, regulating body temperature just like breathing does.

The large intestine

The large intestine is in the lower body cavity; its upper end connects with the small intestine via the ileocaecal valve, and its lower end is the anus. If the chi of the large intestine is flowing smoothly through its meridian, the organ's functions of receiving waste sent from the small intestine, passing water to the bladder to be cleared through urination, and excreting solid waste will all work effectively. If the chi flow becomes blocked, heat could accumulate in the large intestine, causing constipation. Or, if the large intestine chi becomes weak, diarrhoea could result.

More Information

For information on **balancing energy in the lung and large intestine meridians,** see pages 174–175.

PRACTICE

The lung meridian is used to treat all kinds of respiratory disease. As well as healing illness in the large intestine, the large intestine meridian can be used to help with problems concerning the index finger, wrist, elbow, shoulder and head.

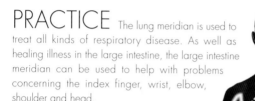

Position of the lungs

Ancient
A meridian image from an ancient Chinese text.

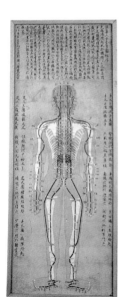

Lung meridian
Points on the lung meridian can be used to treat arthritis or impaired movement of the thumb and damaged biceps, as well as respiratory problems such as asthma, bronchitis and flu. The first point is right over the top of the organ.

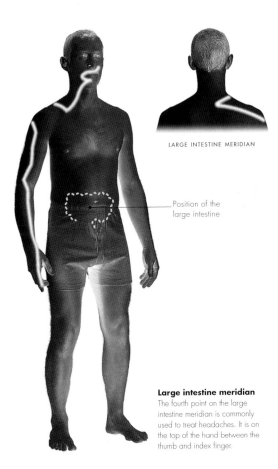

LARGE INTESTINE MERIDIAN

Position of the
large intestine

Large intestine meridian
The fourth point on the large
intestine meridian is commonly
used to treat headaches. It is on
the top of the hand between the
thumb and index finger.

Meridians and Organs: 2

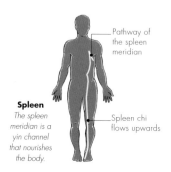

Pathway of the spleen meridian

Spleen
The spleen meridian is a yin channel that nourishes the body.

Spleen chi flows upwards

The stomach

The stomach is in the middle body cavity. Providing that stomach meridian chi is flowing smoothly, it will ensure that food is digested then passed on down to the small intestine.

Chi flows downwards in this meridian; if the flow is reversed, caused by an infection or food poisoning, it could result in nausea or vomiting.

The stomach is connected to the mouth, so food that irritates it will cause mouth ulcers. If the chi flow in the stomach meridian is obstructed, heat could accumulate in the stomach, causing pain, hunger or bad breath.

The spleen

Nutrients from food are extracted in the stomach and given to the spleen, which absorbs them and uses them to make blood and to nourish the body and muscles. The spleen sends nutritional chi up to the lungs to help them keep the defensive chi (a type of chi made from other types of chi) strong. The chi of the spleen meridian flows upwards.

The condition of the spleen and the blood vessels can be observed by looking at the lips. For example, pale lips indicate weak spleen blood.

The spleen also controls the water metabolism, and if this ability is impaired there may be diarrhoea, lassitude, abdominal distension, oedema, or problems with phlegm. The spleen dislikes excessively damp conditions, which can interrupt the workings of the gastrointestinal tract.

The heart

The heart is located in the upper body cavity, slightly to the left side. It pumps the blood through the blood vessels to all parts of the body. If a person suffers from cold hands and feet, it could be due to poor function of the heart muscle.

An internal branch of the heart meridian ascends into the head, through the tongue and eyes and into the brain, so the heart and the mind are connected. When people are excited, heart rate increases; when they are emotionally stressed, their heart becomes stressed. Heat in the heart can cause mental irritability or insomnia.

The tongue is the opening of the heart: if there is heat in the heart, the tip of the tongue will be very red, like a strawberry. The heart is reflected in the face too. If the face is pale, the chi in the heart meridian is insufficient and so the circulation is weak. In summer, excess heat can aggravate the heart and cause the face to be flushed, and may also lead to impatience and irritability.

More Information

For more information on **meridians** see pages 42–43.

PRACTICE

The heart meridian is used to treat poor circulation. The stomach and spleen play major parts in extracting energy from food, and circulating this chi to the heart and lungs through the meridians.

Position of the heart

Acupoint Heart 7

A flowing sequence of chi kung movements called Waving Hands Like Clouds is designed to balance the chi energy in the stomach and spleen meridians and organs (see pages 176–177).

Heart meridian
The Chinese believe that the heart and the emotions are linked. The acupuncture point Heart 7 on the wrist crease can be used to calm the heart and emotions.

Stomach meridian

Points on the stomach meridian on the abdomen are used to heal digestive illnesses. Points on the jaw are used in the healing of toothache. Points on the foot can be used to reduce migraine pain in the head. Local stomach acupoints on the knee are used for knee injuries.

Spleen meridian

The taste associated with the spleen and stomach is sweet. Sweet-tasting herbs, such as dried liquorice root, are used to strengthen the spleen. Anxiety is one problem associated with weakness in the spleen and stomach. People who are anxious often crave sweet things. Beef soup is one thing that can be used to replenish the spleen blood. The best way to help the body stay strong is to eat enough good food often enough, so that the spleen can use it to make sufficient good-quality blood. You are what you eat.

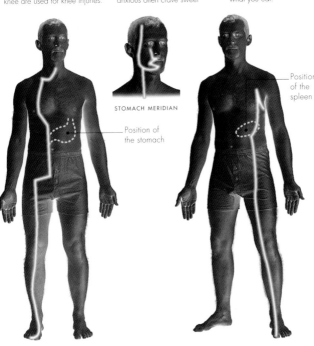

STOMACH MERIDIAN

— Position of the stomach

— Position of the spleen

STOMACH MERIDIAN

SPLEEN MERIDIAN

Meridians and Organs: 3

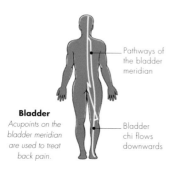

Bladder
Acupoints on the bladder meridian are used to treat back pain.

Pathways of the bladder meridian

Bladder chi flows downwards

The small intestine

The small intestine is located in the lower and middle body cavities. It receives food from the stomach at its top end, which it digests further and passes on to the large intestine at its lower end. If there is an imbalance with the flow of chi through the small intestine meridian, it is likely to give rise to problems with digestion and excretion.

There is a flowing sequence of chi kung movements called Brush Knee and Twist Step, designed to balance the chi energy in the heart and small intestine meridians and organs (see pages 180–183).

The bladder

The bladder is concerned with the regulation of water, or body fluids, in the body, and is paired with the kidneys. It is located in the lower body cavity. It receives waste body fluids from the large and small intestines, which it stores and then discharges as urine. If bladder chi is weak, it can lead to incontinence. If there is heat in or infection of the bladder it can cause pain on urination, infrequent urination, or darker yellow urine.

The kidneys

The kidneys are located in the lower body cavity, on either side of the lumbar vertebrae. They create and store essence (the vital force governing growth, reproduction and development) and are associated with the energy we inherit from our parents. They control the lower body cavity and so influence reproduction and the sexual organs, the bladder and urination. They nourish the bone marrow, spinal fluid and brain, hormones and the blood.

The kidneys regulate water in the body, so we look to them in cases of oedema (as well as to the spleen and lungs). The kidneys dislike the cold and people with bone injuries often complain that when it gets cold their injuries feel worse. The kidneys also control the composition of the bones, so strengthening the kidneys is important to prevent arthritis (see pages 154–155). The teeth are also controlled by the kidneys. If the kidneys' chi is weak, the teeth will easily chip and loosen.

Overwork and illness can consume essence and weaken the kidneys, causing them to ache; also excess loss of seminal essence will cause the kidneys to hurt and become weaker.

The colour associated with the kidneys is black. People with health problems that weaken the kidneys have black rings under their eyes.

More Information

For an exercise to **balance chi energy in the kidney and bladder meridians and organs**, see pages 184–187.

PRACTICE

The small intestine meridian is used to treat upper back, neck and shoulder conditions as well as intestinal diseases. Points on the bladder meridian are used to reinforce the chi of the main internal organs; those on the kidney meridian are used to affect the composition of the bones.

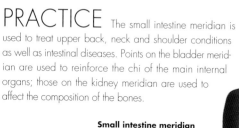

Small intestine meridian
The acupoint Small Intestine 3 is used in conjunction with Bladder point 62 for treating whiplash (see pages 104–107).

Position of the small intestine

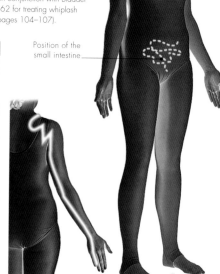

Exercise

There is a flowing sequence of chi kung movements called Brush Knee and Twist Step, designed to balance the chi energy in the heart and small intestine meridians and organs (see pages 182–183).

Bladder meridian

Acupuncturists use the points on the bladder meridian on the back to treat all the main internal organs.

Kidney meridian

In Chinese medicine the kidneys are an extremely important organ because they control our bones and sexual energy.

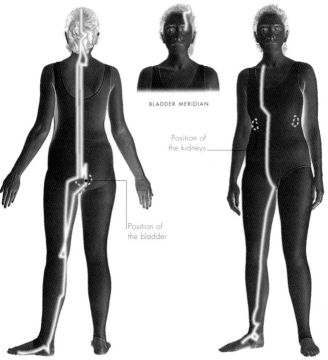

BLADDER MERIDIAN

Position of the kidneys

Position of the bladder

BLADDER MERIDIAN

KIDNEY MERIDIAN

Meridians and Organs:4

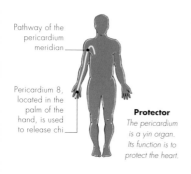

Pathway of the pericardium meridian

Pericardium 8, located in the palm of the hand, is used to release chi

Protector
The pericardium is a yin organ. Its function is to protect the heart.

The pericardium

The chi of the heart can become unbalanced as a result of illness, emotional disturbance, exercise, or injury. The pericardium is the protective outer covering of the heart. Its function is to protect the heart from these pathogenic factors. If there is heat in the heart, there will also be heat in the pericardium. Therefore it is important to maintain an emotionally balanced state, avoiding being disturbed by extremes of emotion, to prevent the heart and pericardium becoming overheated. Chi kung can be used to calm the mind, the heart and the emotions.

The triple warmer

The triple warmer helps move heat around the body. The three warmers are: the upper body cavity (above the solar plexus); the middle body cavity (between the solar plexus and the navel); and the lower body cavity (below the navel). The triple warmer meridian runs through all three body cavities and helps to regulate their temperature. It assists in distributing the essence of the kidneys around the body, helps to distribute body fluids, and is primarily used to disperse the build-up of excess body heat.

The triple warmer meridian connects with the pericardium meridian. Therefore heat that rises up through the body and affects the heart and pericardium can be cleared through the triple warmer meridian.

There is a flowing sequence of chi kung movements called Opening The Gates, designed to balance the chi energy in the pericardium and triple warmer meridians and organs, (see pages 188–191).

The gall bladder

The gall bladder and liver meridians connect. If chi flow is smooth through the gall bladder meridian, its function of receiving the bile produced from old blood in the liver, and secreting it on into the large intestine to help digest food, will work effectively.

The liver

The liver is on the right side of the middle body cavity. If chi flow is smooth through the liver, it will be able to store blood and regulate its flow effectively. The liver is a reservoir of the blood; more blood is released in times of activity and less during rest. We should sleep on the right side of our body so that our blood can get back into the liver easily. The eyes are the opening of the liver. If the liver blood is deficient, eyesight will be weak.

More Information

For information on **healing the liver and gall bladder** see pages 192–195.

PRACTICE

Chi kung exercises can help to balance chi in the pericardium and triple warmer meridians, and to release blockages from the gall bladder meridian, which connects to the liver meridian.

Triple warmer meridian
One of the main uses of the triple warmer meridian is to reduce excess heat in the body from, for example, fever or sunstroke. The main point used is Triple Warmer 5 (see page 104).

Pericardium meridian
Acupoint Pericardium 8 in the palm of the hand is used to emit chi when practising the martial or healing arts.

Posit on of t
pericardium

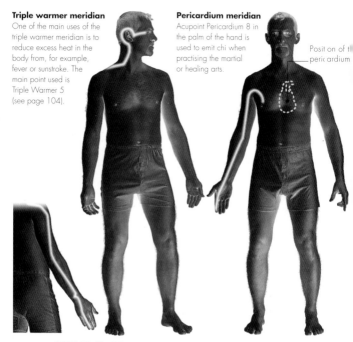

TRIPLE WARMER MERIDIAN

PERICARDIUM MERIDIAN

Gall bladder meridian

This meridian controls the vertical movement of chi in the body.

GALL BLADDER MERIDIAN

Liver meridian

An unseen pathway goes to the head and affects the eyes.

Position of the liver

Exercise

A chi kung movement sequence, called Step Back and Repulse Monkey, is designed to balance the chi energy in the liver and gall bladder meridians and organs (see pages 192–195).

GALL BLADDER MERIDIAN

LIVER MERIDIAN

Meridians and Organs:5

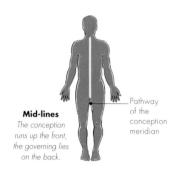

Mid-lines
The conception runs up the front, the governing lies on the back.

Pathway of the conception meridian

The conception meridian

The conception meridian runs along the mid-line of the front of the body, from the perineum all the way up the torso and neck to the end of the middle of the lower gum. If the chi in this meridian is flowing freely, it is able to supply all the yin meridians in the whole body. The conception meridian is considered to be a huge lake of water that flows down the yin meridians and nourishes all the internal organs. It is rather like rain falling on crops and making them grow. It is the yin meridians that are most concerned with nourishing and regenerating the

body, and the conception meridian plays a vital role in the development of the baby in the womb. Its pathway often becomes visible in pregnant women, from the pubic region up to the navel. At this time it looks like a dark line.

There are many points on the conception meridian that lie directly over various internal organs, and so can be used to control the activity of these. If an organ is overactive, which is known as a yang state, the amount of chi in that acupuncture point needs to be reduced. If an organ is weak and underactive, which is known as a yin state, the amount of chi in that point should be increased.

The governing meridian

The governing meridian runs along the mid-line of the back of the body, from the coccyx all the way up the spine and over the head, and ends in the middle of the upper gum. If the chi in this meridian is flowing freely, it is able to keep all the yang meridians in the whole body well supplied with chi.

The governing meridian is like the sun, radiating light along all the yang meridians and providing power to all the internal organs. It is the yang meridians that are most concerned with defending the body against attack from exogenous pathogenic factors such as viruses, bacteria, and extreme weather conditions. In the summer, the hot sun can cause dehydration, heatstroke, and even death. In winter, the cold can cause hypothermia and death. So having a sufficient supply of good, strong chi flowing in the yang meridians, supplied by the governing meridian, is essential for survival.

Later in this book you will find many exercises that strengthen the spine, a part of the governing meridian. Also, all nerves have their roots in the spine, so a healthy spine is very important for our overall general health.

More Information

For information on **healing the spine** see pages 162–169.

PRACTICE

The governing and conception meridians are also referred to as "vessels" because they can store a vast amount of essence and energy. When they have abundant chi, it flows into all the other meridians.

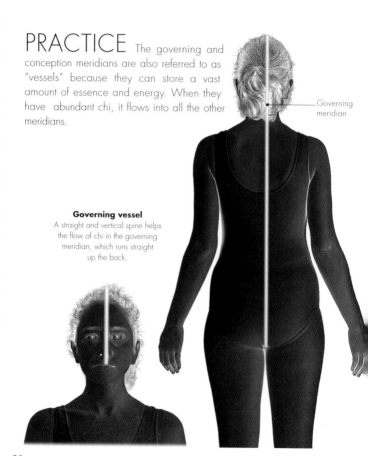

Governing meridian

Governing vessel
A straight and vertical spine helps the flow of chi in the governing meridian, which runs straight up the back.

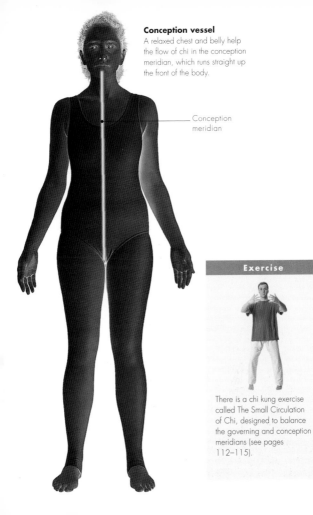

Conception vessel

A relaxed chest and belly help the flow of chi in the conception meridian, which runs straight up the front of the body.

Conception meridian

Exercise

There is a chi kung exercise called The Small Circulation of Chi, designed to balance the governing and conception meridians (see pages 112–115).

The Acupuncture Energy Points

The governor

The governing vessel supplies yang meridians throughout the body.

The energy points used in acupuncture, also called meridian points, are the points of high electric conductance on the meridians, where the flow of chi can be influenced most easily. If the electrical resistance of the skin is measured, all these energy points are shown to have a lower resistance than the surrounding skin. In 1991, experiments were carried out with a Superconducting Quantum Interference Device to map the lines of the force fields of electromagnetic energy generated by the human body. These were found to correspond exactly with the acupuncture meridians and acupuncture points which were documented by the Chinese over 5,000 years ago.

Physical illness

A wide variety of physical ailments can be healed by rebalancing chi in the meridians, because the physical body and meridian system are interdependent and interconnected. It is possible to influence the activity of the internal organs of the torso through the application of acupuncture or acupressure to the energy points on the surface of the body.

During chi kung practice, the acupuncture points can be pressed and rubbed in a clockwise or anticlockwise direction to reduce or reinforce the flow of chi in the meridians, and so help to heal the body.

In our chi kung practice we can also initiate the healing effect associated with a specific point by concentrating on it. This will increase the chi at that point, because chi also responds to the power of the mind. We can lead the chi around our bodies, through mental effort, in order to cure disease and improve health. Additionally, we can extend chi beyond our own body and into other people to heal them.

Using acupuncture points

Practitioners of healing arts such as acupuncture use the points to heal patients. Practitioners of martial arts such as tai chi strike opponents' points to defeat them. Chi kung practitioners, on the other hand, lead chi along the meridians in order to heal themselves.

More Information

For information on **healing chi** see pages 108–111.

ENERGY POINTS
In our chi kung practice there are a few acupuncture points that we use constantly: Kidney 1, Pericardium 8, Governing 20, Conception 4 and Conception 6. It is important to be familiar with these before starting chi kung training.

Kidney 1
Kidney 1 (K-1), on the sole of the foot, is used to draw the energy of the earth into the body.

Pericardium 8
Pericardium 8 (P-8), in the palm of the hand, is used to release chi into the body (or another person) for healing.

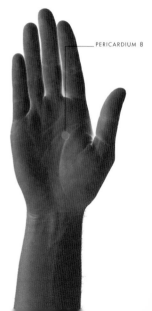

PERICARDIUM 8

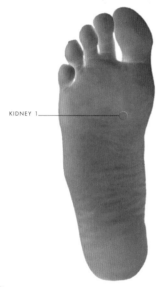

KIDNEY 1

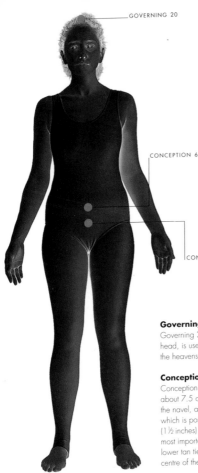

GOVERNING 20

CONCEPTION 6

CONCEPTION 4

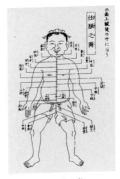

Ancient healing
Archaeologists have found evidence of acupuncture practice dating from 1000BC.

Governing 20

Governing 20 (G-20), on the top of the head, is used to draw in energy from the heavens, sun, moon, and stars.

Conception 4 and 6

Conception 4 (C-4), which is located about 7.5 centimetres (3 inches) below the navel, and Conception 6 (C-6), which is positioned 4 centimetres (1½ inches) below the navel, are the most important points for accessing the lower tan tien energy centre in the centre of the belly (see pages 60–63).

Tan Tien Energy Centres

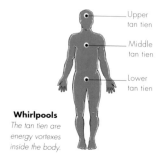

Upper
tan tien

Middle
tan tien

Lower
tan tien

Whirlpools
*The tan tien are
energy vortexes
inside the body.*

There are three key energy centres in the body, each called a *tan tien*, which means "field of the elixir of life". The concept of the tan tien originated in ancient times: the Chinese used the word "field" to convey the idea that life energy can be cultivated within the body in the same way that a crop can be cultivated in a field. A crop will only flourish if all the factors are right: the ground has to be good, just as the physical body needs to be strong, and the right crops need to be planted, emphasizing the importance of a good diet and positive thoughts. The Chinese saw themselves as a part of

nature. They believed that external environmental factors had parallels inside the body, which could lead to ill-health if they became unbalanced. They observed that when the sun was strong in summer, it caused drought and crop failure; likewise they knew that inside the body this same heat could cause dehydration, heatstroke, and death. If the rains were heavy there was a possibility of flooding; in the body, an excess of water could cause oedema. If there was not enough sunlight (chi) in the body, cold winter weather could cause hypothermia and death.

The power of the elements

The Chinese referred to the elemental forces from above as "heaven". The elements were in themselves potential killers, but they could also destroy human life by destroying food crops. From these observations the Chinese deduced that man was affected by heaven. The crops in the earth required sunlight and rain to grow, so earth also relied on heaven, and man was dependent on the food from the earth. They concluded that heaven, earth, and man were interconnected and continuously affected by one another, and that in order to live a long and healthy life, man needed to curb the excesses of his own nature, balance his internal environment, and be in tune with the natural world around him.

The lower tan tien energy centre is located just below and behind the navel and is associated with the earth and water. This energy centre is where the chi for action comes from. The middle tan tien is situated behind the solar plexus and is associated with the sun and fire. This is easily affected by the emotions. The upper tan tien lies behind the mid-point between the eyebrows and is associated with heaven. This is the energy centre where all thoughts are received.

More Information

For more information on **the energy centres** see pages 62–63.

ENERGY CENTRES

The body's three tan tien energy centres are located on the thrusting channel, which runs up the centre of the body (see pages 128–131). It is beneficial for students of chi kung to spend their first few years of practice concentrating on achieving balance and stability in their lower tan tien.

Spirit
The spirit is nourished in the lower tan tien (see page 208) and released from the upper tan tien (see page 210).

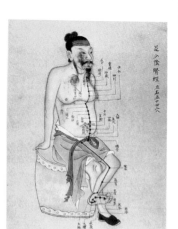

Meridians
The ideas of meridians and energy centres are interrelated.

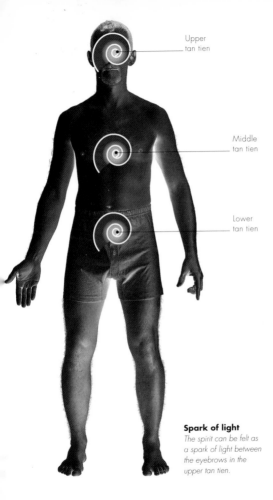

Upper
tan tien

Middle
tan tien

Lower
tan tien

Spark of light

*The spirit can be felt as
a spark of light between
the eyebrows in the
upper tan tien.*

Moving Energy With Your Mind

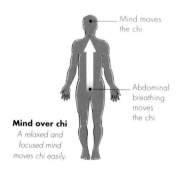

Mind moves the chi

Abdominal breathing moves the chi

Mind over chi
A relaxed and focused mind moves chi easily.

In chi kung, chi is moved through different meridians to nourish and heal the internal organs, so that we can be strong and live long lives. We use the mind to move the chi, either by telling the body to adopt a certain posture, which activates a particular meridian, or by instructing the body to breathe a special way, which will boost the amount of chi in the body and invigorate its movement.

There is also another, more direct, way. With the mind's power of sustained concentration and its ability to

focus, we are able to lead chi through the meridian system and target specific points. The way that the mind leads chi is rather like an arrow with a thread attached to it. When a marksman concentrates on the bull's-eye of a target, he uses his external vision to focus on a point outside himself, so that when the arrow is released, it will go straight to the bull's-eye. In our chi kung energy work, we use our internal "mind's eye" to focus on points inside ourselves and lead the chi to them.

Exercises such as Leading the Chi Through The 12 Main Meridians With the Power of the Mind (see pages 108–111), The Small Circulation of Chi (see pages 112–115), The Big Circulation of Chi (see pages 126–127), and The Thrusting Channel Circulation Through The Three Tan Tiens (see pages 128–131), help us to stay healthy by using the mind to move the chi, which in turn moves blood and other body fluids around the body.

Regular practice

Through regular practice the power of our mind increases and we can control our internal energy and our emotions more easily. Once this is achieved, we are quickly able to improve our lives – we are able to make choices that are based on what is best and most appropriate, rather than on avoiding our fears and being a slave to our desires. For example, for many men the desire for sexual satisfaction is often a powerful driving force in their decisions. It sometimes happens that what they think, say, and do is inappropriate because they are unable to control their sexual energy. On pages 134–145 there are exercises that enable us to use the power of our mind to control the movement of sexual energy.

More Information

For more information on **moving chi with the mind** see pages 108–111.

EXERCISES FOR ENERGY

Practised by millions of Chinese every day, chi kung exercises increase energy and encourage its smooth circulation around the body to improve health on all levels – physically, mentally, emotionally, and, eventually, spiritually. ❧ We begin with breathing exercises and various postures. Then we move on to exercises that may seem somewhat intangible, for example moving energy around the body with the power of the mind. Finally, we deal with the more abstract aspect of ourselves: the spirit. ❧ In the West the importance of cardiovascular and aerobic exercise is stressed, whereas the Chinese emphasize the importance of chi flow through the meridian system. A Western cultural perspective is not a barrier to reaping the benefits of chi kung, however. Chi kung is not a religion; it is an exercise system that can benefit everyone.

Chi Kung Breathing

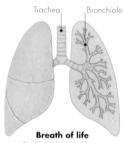

Trachea   Bronchiole

Breath of life
*Chi kung breathing boosts
the defensive chi.*

The special abdominal breathing that is practised in chi kung can regulate the body, mind, emotions, energy, and spirit, all of which are interconnected. Most people already know that taking a deep breath through the nose and exhaling slowly through the mouth helps to reduce stress, demonstrating that regulating the breath can exert a calming effect on a restless mind and untamed emotions.

Chi kung abdominal breathing activates the lower tan tien energy centre located in the centre of the belly, and enables chi to travel from there to all the other parts of the body. These breathing exercises help generate and pump chi around the body, as well as massaging and strengthening the internal organs.

Chi kung breathing is usually practised in various standing postures initially – The Mother Posture, The Father Posture, The Daughter Posture, and The Son Posture (see pages 72–87).

Different types of breathing

There are four different types of chi kung abdominal breathing. The first is upper abdominal breathing, which strengthens acquired chi (chi from food and air). The second is reverse lower abdominal breathing, which strengthens inherited chi and essence. The third type is wave breathing, combining upper abdominal and reverse lower abdominal breathing. The fourth type is called tortoise breathing, and is a very slow version of wave breathing, which has a pause between inhalation and exhalation, and another pause between exhalation and inhalation.

On inhalation, wave and tortoise breathing cause the inherited chi and essence of the lower abdomen to be brought up to the upper abdomen where they can be mixed with the acquired chi and made stronger. Then, on exhalation, they return to the lower abdomen to consolidate the strength and vitality of the lower tan tien energy centre. However, if you are a beginner, you should only use upper abdominal breathing. As your technique improves, you will be able to build up to more advanced breathing techniques.

Chi kung breathing pumps the body with chi, strengthening the internal energy and, in turn, defensive energy. This will increase your body's resistance to viruses, bacteria, and adverse weather conditions. In time, chi kung breathing will become automatic, both while awake and asleep.

More Information

For more information on chi kung breathing see pages 70–71.

CHI KUNG BREATHING

This is accomplished by mental intention, not by muscle tension, so do not force anything. Keep the mouth closed, with the tongue touching the roof of the mouth, and breathe through the nose slowly and calmly. The chest should be relaxed while the abdomen is expanded and contracted by the inhalation and exhalation of breath. Breathe very quietly so that you cannot even hear yourself breathe.

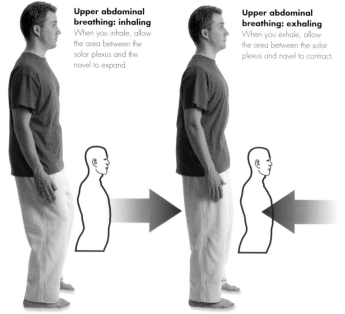

Upper abdominal breathing: inhaling
When you inhale, allow the area between the solar plexus and the navel to expand.

Upper abdominal breathing: exhaling
When you exhale, allow the area between the solar plexus and navel to contract.

Reverse lower abdominal breathing: inhaling
When you inhale, allow the area between the navel and the pubic bone to contract.

Reverse lower abdominal breathing: exhaling
When you exhale, allow the area between the navel and the pubic bone to expand.

The Mother Posture

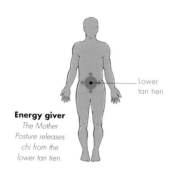

Lower tan tien

Energy giver
The Mother Posture releases chi from the lower tan tien.

The Mother Posture is a still, standing posture that is held for 15 minutes to release chi from the lower tan tien energy centre into the rest of the body. It is followed by the Father, Daughter and Son postures.

Exercise

Place your feet about 2.5 centimetres (1 inch) more than shoulder-width apart, with the insides of the feet parallel. The body weight should be right over the acupuncture point Stomach 41 (S-41), where the front of the shin bone meets the top of the foot. The feet should arch slightly, so that the instep and the point

Kidney 1 (K-1) are just off the ground (see page 58). Slightly bend the knees and push them outwards a little. Tuck the sacrum under the body to straighten the lower back in the area of the lumbar vertebrae.

Pull the chin in and lift the back of the head up so that the whole spine is straight and vertical. Place the tongue on the roof of the mouth.

Position your arms out in front of you in a horseshoe shape (do not lock the elbows), as if hugging a large tree. Open the hands, with the palms towards you and the skin between the thumb and index finger stretched straight. Keep the hands concave, as if you are holding a football. Point the fingers up at a slight diagonal angle and make sure they do not touch each other. The hands should be yin (palm is slightly compressed and the back of the hand slightly stretched). A yin hand releases yang chi energy.

There should be a big space under the arms, which are held almost 90 degrees away from the body. The elbows are a fraction below the height of the shoulders and the hands are at the height of the neck, about 5–7.5 centimetres (2–3 inches) away from each other. Relax, and look straight ahead at a distant horizon. Empty your mind.

The body, and in particular the shoulders and belly, should be as relaxed as possible. This leads to a feeling of fullness in the belly, and when the internal organs finally also relax, the chi flow triggers various internal secretions and gurglings from the belly.

Return the chi to the lower tan tien and store it there after the exercise (see pages 88–95) or start the next posture.

During the first few months of chi kung, simply hold this posture; later you can start to practise the four types of chi kung breathing as well. Don't rush to do everything – benefits that are accumulated slowly last longer.

More information

For information on **breathing** see pages 68–71.

MOTHER POSTURE

This posture can be practised by itself, or as the first in a sequence of postures to release the chi into different parts of the body. In this posture, different things happen to each person; however, experiences follow a general order. To begin with, you will probably feel a warm glow spreading outwards from the belly. It will push the cold ahead of it, so at first your hands will feel cold, then just the fingers, then just the fingertips, and eventually the whole body will be warm. The body feels as though it is sinking into the earth while the spirit floats up to the sky. It is as if you are there and not there at the same time, feeling heavy below and light above. You are inside yourself, and you also expand outside yourself. Your consciousness is split between your physical body and your spirit body: you can look down from a height and see yourself standing there.

Hand Position

The hands are open but not tensed. The thumbs and fingers do not touch each other.

MOTHER

Put the mind in the lower tan tien

Keep the hands up by using the power of mental intention, not muscle tension

Relax the belly

Free-flowing chi

Where chi is blocked, you will experience an aching or shaking. As the flow of chi increases, these feelings will clear. A gentle rocking backwards and forwards will eventually develop. With men, the body will circle slightly in a clockwise movement; with women it will be an anticlockwise movement. Tingling in the fingertips and on the top of the head may also be sensed. Eventually, the hands and whole body will become surrounded by an electromagnetic force field.

The Father Posture

Strong shoulders
The Father Posture moves the chi through the shoulders.

The Father Posture brings chi energy flooding through the shoulder joints, upper back and neck, so it is useful for treating problems such as whiplash, frozen shoulder, or a traumatic injury to the neck. It works on the heart and small intestine meridians because it flexes the tendons that they run along, right to the ends of the little and ring fingers.

Exercise

This posture is exactly the same as The Mother Posture, except that the hands are turned over and slanted diagonally, with the thumb closest to you, so that you see the backs of the fingers, with the little finger furthest away at the top.

In The Mother Posture the hands were slightly yin and in this, the hands are slightly yang. A yang hand has the palm slightly stretched and the back of the hand compressed. A yang hand releases yin chi energy. In still chi kung postures such as these, we are not so aware of the activity of yin and yang chi. However, in the chi kung movement sequences later in the book, this is a very important part of each exercise.

Return the chi to the lower tan tien and store it there when you have finished the exercise (see pages 88–95).

Poetry and chi kung

A selection of meditative poetry is included in this book to help you to cultivate a chi kung frame of mind.

BEFORE THE UNIVERSE IS CREATED

It is soundless and formless

*The body must be
as transparent as air*

*Follow the way of nature
Like the chime of a big bell*

*That hangs from the ceiling
of an old temple*

LI TAO TZE

FATHER POSTURE

This is exactly the same as The Mother Posture, except for the position of the hands. It could be used as a single posture to heal the shoulders, or it could be next in sequence after The Mother Posture, each posture being held for 15 minutes. If it is part of a sequence, do not drop the hands but just turn them over. As you begin to turn them, inhale; as you finish turning them, exhale. You can, of course, also practise the four types of chi kung breathing in this posture. As with The Mother Posture, you will experience an aching and shaking where chi is blocked. When the flow of chi increases, these feelings will cease.

Hand Position

The palms should face away from the body, with the thumbs closest to you and the little fingers at the top, furthest away. The heart and small intestine meridians in the little and ring fingers are activated by the flexing created by this posture.

FATHER

78

Empty your
mind of
thought

The little finger
feels slightly flexed

Fill your belly
with chi

Imagine
a spring
pushing out
just above
the knees

1 *Stand with your feet about
2.5 centimetres (1 inch) more
than shoulder-width apart.*

2 *Bend the knees slightly and
push them outwards a little.
Tuck the sacrum under the body.*

3 *Pull the chin in and lift up the
back of the head. Hold the arms
out in front of you in the shape
of a horseshoe.*

4 *Open the hands, with the
palms away from you, the thumbs
closest to you and little fingers
at the top, furthest away. Look
straight ahead at a distant
horizon and empty your mind.
Hold for 15 minutes.*

The Daughter Posture

Sturdy arms

The Daughter Posture moves the chi through the elbows and forearms.

The Daughter Posture brings chi energy through the elbow joints and along the forearms. This means that the posture is useful for treating tennis elbow and some types of carpal tunnel syndrome (CTS), as well as repetitive strain injury (RSI) caused by typing. The posture is used both as a preventive measure and to heal damage that has already occurred.

Exercise

The Daughter Posture is exactly the same as The Mother Posture, except that the arms are positioned a little lower, at about the height of the solar plexus. As for the previous postures, keep space under the arms, as if there is a football there. Turn the hands palm down and inwards slightly, so that the thumb and index fingers make a diamond shape. The hands are also slightly yin-shaped.

This posture can be practised alone, or as part of a sequence. When you have finished the exercise, return the chi to the lower tan tien and store it there (see pages 88–95).

Wu chi

When practising any type of chi kung, your mind and body should enter into a state of wu chi. This is a state in which you feel calm and centred, as well as being balanced and aware. Your body should feel as though it is being held up by the expanded energy you have created inside you.

TAO TE CHING

A form without an object
It is elusive and fleeting
Run into it and not see its face
Follow it and not see its back
Use the way of the ancients
to master the present

LAO TZU

DAUGHTER POSTURE

This exercise could be used as a single posture to heal the elbows and forearms, or it could be the next in sequence after The Mother and Father Postures, each posture being held for 15 minutes. If it is part of a sequence, inhale as you move the arms to their new position and exhale when they are at the height of the solar plexus. You can, of course, also practise the four types of chi kung breathing in this posture. The fingertips will feel warm and full as chi and blood rush to the hands. The hands will become warm, heavy and soft, but as dense as lead.

Hand Position

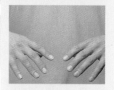

The hands should be turned palm down and slightly inwards. The chi will feel like warm water gently rolling downhill as it runs down the forearms into the hands.

DAUGHTER

Let the arms hang from the shoulders like branches from a tree trunk

Hands are slightly yin-shaped

1 *Stand with your feet about 2.5 cm (1 inch) more than shoulder-width apart.*

2 *Bend the knees slightly and push them outwards a little. Tuck the sacrum under the body.*

3 *Pull the chin in and lift up the back of the head.*

4 *Position the arms out in front of you, lower than in The Mother Posture, at about solar plexus height. Turn the palms down and slightly inwards .*

5 *Look straight ahead, at a distant horizon, and empty your mind. Hold for 15 minutes.*

Feet should be shoulder-width apart

The Son Posture

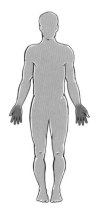

Capable hands
The Son Posture moves chi into the wrists and hands.

T he Son Posture brings chi energy pulsing through the wrist joints and into the hands, so it is useful for treating carpal tunnel syndrome, repetitive strain injury, arthritis of the hands and fingers, and circulatory problems that cause cold extremities. It can be used both as a means of helping to heal these conditions and to prevent them occurring.

Exercise

The Son Posture is exactly the same as The Daughter Posture, except that the palms face each other and the hands are slightly yang, pointing downwards a fraction. There must be a space of about 11 centimetres (4 inches) between the hands, with both Pericardium 8 (P-8) points facing each other.

Return the chi to the lower tan tien and store it there when you have completed the entire exercise (see pages 88–95).

Charging up the hands for healing

While standing in The Son Posture, there is an extra chi kung exercise that can be practised. Your hands will become charged with chi. This creates a strong sensation, as if you are holding a ball of warm, electromagnetic energy between your hands.

As you inhale, try to pull your hands apart, but imagine they are being pulled together like magnets attracting each other. The hands should move only

2.5 centimetres (1 inch) away from each other. As you exhale, try and squeeze your hands together but imagine that they are being pushed apart, like magnets repelling each other. The hands then move back to their original position.

When the hands move towards each other they will form a yang shape, and when they move away from each other they will become yin-shaped. However in both cases, they never actually touch each other.

Eventually, with practice, the sensation of chi increases and you physically move the hands less and less, until to outward appearances they are not moving at all but inside they are pulsing and buzzing, vibrating and humming. This would be a good time to heal a sick or injured part of your body (or someone else's) by touch.

More Information

For information on using **healing hands on the kidneys** see pages 154–155

SON POSTURE

This exercise mirrors The Daughter Posture, except that the palms face each other and the hands are slightly yang, pointing downwards a fraction. It could be used as a single exercise to heal the wrist joints and hands, or it could be performed as the next in sequence after The Mother, Father, and Daughter Postures, with each being held for 15 minutes. If it is part of a sequence, inhale as you begin to turn the hands and exhale when they face each other. The four types of chi kung breathing can be practised in this posture.

Turn the palms to face each other and point the hands down slightly. When the hands are charged with chi, you will feel as though you are holding a glowing ball of healing energy.

SON

It is vital to keep space under the arms. Closing up the shoulder joint would reduce the chi flow in the arms and upper body

1 Stand with your feet about 2.5 centimetres (1 inch) more than shoulder-width apart.

2 Bend the knees slightly and push them outwards a little. Tuck the sacrum under the body.

3 Pull the chin in and lift up the back of the head.

4 Position the arms out in front of you, lower than in The Mother Posture, at about solar plexus height. Turn the palms to face each other and point the hands down slightly.

5 Look straight ahead, at a distant horizon, and empty your mind. Hold for 15 minutes.

Bringing Energy to the Lower Tan Tien

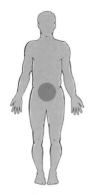

Chi store
It is vital to bring chi into the belly after chi kung exercise.

I cannot stress enough how important it is to bring the chi back down into the belly after any chi kung exercise. If we do not there are many possible side-effects, such as excessive heat in the heart and brain, which will cause migraines, headaches, restlessness, insomnia, overactive thinking and irrational thinking, as well as a tendency to feel over-emotional. There is also the possibility of excessive blood heat accumulating. This could cause circulatory problems, including stagnation and coagulation of the blood.

After chi kung exercise, chi becomes hot because we have activated it and invigorated it with our chi kung breathing. Bringing the chi energy to the lower tan tien and storing it there does not involve this special breathing, so the chi can cool down.

In order to do this, we must bring the hot chi into the belly where the cool essence of the kidneys and lower tan tien can help it to condense into essence (the vital force governing growth, reproduction and development), which can be used by the body to nourish the internal organs, including the spine and brain.

Activity is yang and creates chi; calmness is yin and creates essence. In general, hot chi flows along the yang meridians to increase functional power in the body, and cool chi (essence) flows along the yin meridians to nourish and regenerate the body.

Inner city blues

In the Western world about 90 per cent of people live in cities, which tend to be polluted and cause people to live very stressful lives. This super-fast, high-stress way of living overheats the body. If you are a city-dweller, it is important to centre yourself in the belly, become calm and steady, and cool down your hot chi, overactive mind and emotions.

People who "overdo it", that is, who work and socialize too hard, are said to "burn out" eventually. This is not just a figure of speech – it is a literal description of how excessive yang causes deficient yin.

More Information

For information on **attaining calm** see pages 98–99.

GATHERING THE CHI

After any chi kung exercise it is vital to bring chi back down into the belly or, more specifically, the lower tan tien. The method for achieving this is shown here. There is no set time for holding this position – it will vary from day to day and individual to individual. If you have been very busy and active recently, the chi will take longer to descend to the lower belly. To gauge whether you have held this posture long enough, you need to become aware of what you feel in the belly. When chi has gathered there, it feels like the belly is full and substantial. There is a very strong sensation of your centre of gravity being very low: your belly is full but your head is empty. You will also experience feelings of strength and confidence, as if you could undertake any task and be assured of success.

TAN TIEN

The head is emptied of thought and the mind is serene

The heart and emotions are calm and at ease

The belly is full of chi, blood and essence, which makes you feel sturdy and strong

1 Connect the tips of your thumbs and the two index and middle fingers. Curl in the little and ring fingers so they do not touch anything.

2 Point the peak of the thumb tips up, keeping them level with the height of the navel. The tips of the index and middle fingers point downwards and you should feel very slight pressure between the hands.

3 Position the hands about 18–20 centimetres (7–8 inches) in front of the belly and right over the access points for the lower tan tien, Conception 4 (C-4), which is located 7.5 centimetres (3 inches) below the navel, and Conception 6 (C-6), which is 4 centimetres (1½ inches) below the navel.

4 Relax the belly so that it can expand and draw the chi into it. Don't force it out, just relax and let go.

Storing Energy in the Lower Tan Tien

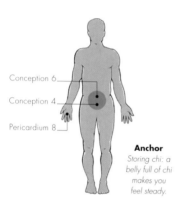

Conception 6

Conception 4

Pericardium 8

Anchor
Storing chi: a belly full of chi makes you feel steady.

This exercise follows the previous one and ensures that chi is successfully stored. There is no special breathing and the belly remains relaxed and full. The process is different for men and women, as men are more yang and women more yin.

Exercise

Men should place acupuncture point Pericardium 8 (P-8), on the palm of the left hand, on Conception 4 (C-4), which is 7.5 centimetres (3 inches) below the navel, or Conception 6 (C-6), which is located 4 centimetres (1½ inches) below the navel. Then the palm of the right hand should be placed on the back of the left hand.

For women, acupuncture point Pericardium 8 (P-8), on the palm of the right hand, is positioned on top of Conception 4 (C-4) or Conception 6 (C-6), which are sited 7.5 and 4 centimetres (3 and 1½ inches) below the navel. The palm of the left hand is placed on the back of the right hand.

Both men and women now need to concentrate on the centre of the lower belly, the centre of the lower tan tien, in particular on a point on the thrusting meridian that forms a vertical line rising from the perineum to the top of the head. To locate the correct point, imagine a line going from Governing 4 (G-4), which is located below lumbar vertebra number two, forwards to Conception 4 (C-4). The point where this almost horizontal line crosses the thrusting meridian is the one we concentrate on. Imagine energy spiralling around this point, like a whirlpool of starlight. Stay relaxed – the key to chi kung is the avoidance of all unnecessary tension.

When chi is stored in the lower tan tien, the belly might expand slightly, or feel more substantial. This produces a calm, happy feeling and a warmth in the tan tien. At this point you can also think positive thoughts, such as, "I feel powerful and peaceful, balanced and calm deep down inside myself". Alternatively, empty your mind.

Storing chi in the lower tan tien energy centre nourishes the internal organs and boosts the immune system.

More Information

For information on the **location of points** see page 115.

STORING ENERGY

When you have finished a chi kung exercise and you have brought the resultant chi energy down to the lower tan tien, the following exercise can be used to ensure that the chi is successfully stored there. The exercise varies slightly depending on whether you are a man or a woman. This is because men are slightly more yang and women a little more yin. It is important to remember that it is vital, in all aspects of chi kung, to avoid all unnecessary tension, and it is particularly important to remain calm and relaxed while performing this exercise.

Hand Positions

Because men are yang, they should place their right hand on top of their left.

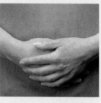

Because women are yin, they should place their left hand on top of their right.

For men
Men should place the acupuncture point Pericardium 8 (P-8), on the palm of the left hand, on top of Conception 4 (C-4) or Conception 6 (C-6). Place the palm of the right hand on the back of the left hand.

For women
Women should place the acupuncture point Pericardium 8 (P-8), on the palm of the right hand, on top of Conception 4 (C-4) or Conception 6 (C-6).

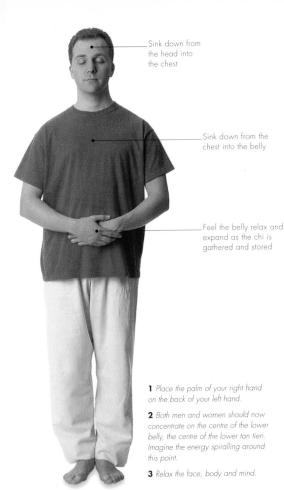

Sink down from the head into the chest

Sink down from the chest into the belly

Feel the belly relax and expand as the chi is gathered and stored

1 *Place the palm of your right hand on the back of your left hand.*

2 *Both men and women should now concentrate on the centre of the lower belly, the centre of the lower tan tien. Imagine the energy spiralling around this point.*

3 *Relax the face, body and mind.*

The Wu Chi Posture

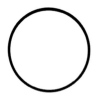

Wholeness
*Wu chi (unity) is symbolized
by an empty circle.*

This posture is practised completely by itself. It is not part of the previous sequence, and we do not practise any special chi kung breathing with it. Nor do we concentrate on anything or try to do anything. This posture is about non-interference with things, and allows whatever is supposed to become apparent to be revealed. This may sound somewhat vague, but that is because the experience will be different for each person. The state of wu chi is a spiritual dimension in which you become aware that not only are you interconnected to the world, but that it is within you as much as you are within it.

Wu chi is symbolized by the empty circle. In this posture you become like an empty vessel that can be filled. Maybe you will be filled with energy or perhaps with good ideas. The Wu Chi Posture puts people into a receptive state so that they open up to new ideas and innovations.

Exercise

The Wu Chi Posture is exactly the same as The Mother Posture, but with the palms of the hands facing towards you and the fingers pointing down. The arms are held out in front of the body, a little lower than the other postures, and to the sides. The hands are slightly yin-shaped. There is space under the arms and, above all else, stillness and calmness are the most important factors.

Being, not doing

You cannot try to enter a state of wu chi, because it is a way of being, not something that you do. Wu chi is essentially our true nature – which is why we are called human *beings*.

TAO TELLING

It has no name,
to speak of it is to lose it

Before heaven and earth
were born it was there

All of existence returns to it

Mysterious and deep, it has no limits
and is the gateway to all wonders

LAO TZU

WU CHI POSTURE

When muddy water is stirred up, everything is obscured. If the water is left to become still, the mud will settle to the bottom and the water will become clear. When the mind and emotions are active, they can resemble water that has been stirred up. If we hope to have clarity and vision in our lives, we must occasionally stand in The Wu Chi Posture and let everything become still and calm. The posture is held until you receive whatever it is that you need – perhaps more chi or some information or motivation. It may take five minutes or 20 minutes. Store the chi and then do whatever you have been guided to do. Or, if you have received some information, quickly write it down.

WU CHI

Still, calm and receptive

Hand Position

Turn the palms to face each other and point the hands down slightly. When the hands are charged with chi, you will feel as though you are holding a glowing ball of healing energy.

Hands are slightly yin-shaped

1 The Wu Chi Posture is exactly the same as The Mother Posture (see pages 72–75), but with the palms of the hands facing towards you and the fingers pointing down.

2 Hold the arms out in front of the body, a little lower than the other postures, and to the sides. The hands are slightly yin-shaped. There is still space under the arms. Above all else, stillness and calmness are the most important factors.

The Immortal Points The Way To Heaven Posture

Digital power
The index finger buzzes with chi.

This posture concentrates chi in both index fingers, charging them up in preparation for manipulating acupuncture points. You can massage the points without charging your hands, but the process will be less effective.

Exercise

Begin in The Son Posture and practise Charging Up The Hands for Healing. Then lift the hands up and move into .

The Mother Posture. Now turn the palms away from you and make the hand sign of The Immortal Points the Way to Heaven. To do this, point the index fingers straight up and curl in the thumb and other fingers, ensuring they do not touch each other or the hand. As you move the arms out to the sides of the body, straighten them very slowly. The energy sensations in the index finger will get stronger and stronger as the hands move to the sides.

When the hands are almost as far as they can go, hold them there. Then begin chi kung breathing: tortoise type is best, but do whatever you can.

Slowly bring the arms back to The Mother Posture. Now you can press the acupuncture points in order to promote healing processes.

More Information

For information on **charging up the hands for healing** see pages 84–85.

IMMORTAL

*Immortal I wander in these
jade-green hills*

*No one can tell
the stillness in my heart*

*My body idles
like a floating cloud*

*Soon I will be free
of this mortal realm*

THE IMMORTAL TAOIST

POINTING TO HEAVEN POSTURE

This posture will help you to "charge up" your hands by concentrating chi in the index fingers, so that you can manipulate acupuncture points more effectively. The posture creates an almost unbearably strong sensation in the index finger.

1 *Begin in The Son Posture and practise Charging Up The Hands for Healing. Then lift the hands up and move into The Mother Posture. Don't rise up – stay low and steady.*

Hand Position

Point the index fingers straight up and curl in the thumb and other fingers, ensuring they do not touch each other or the hand.

IMMORTAL

Try to point your index finger straight up

The arms are straightened out, almost locked in position

Keep the belly relaxed

2 Turn the palms away from you and make the hand sign of The Immortal Points the Way to Heaven. To do this, point the index fingers straight up and curl in the thumb and other fingers, ensuring they do not touch each other or the hand.

3 Straighten the arms slightly as you move them, very slowly, out to the sides of the body. When the hands are almost as far as they can go, hold them there. Then begin chi kung breathing. Slowly bring the arms back to The Mother Posture.

Pressing Points for Health

Ancient guide
The Pa Kua includes eight trigrams that provide a group of commonly used acupuncture points.

There are over 400 basic points used in acupuncture, either individually or in combination. I'm using a group called The Eight Trigram Paired Points as an example. However, for acupuncture treatment, a larger range of points would be used for a greater healing effect. The eight trigrams come from an ancient symbol called the Pa Kua, from the I Ching (see page 14).

The Eight Trigram Paired Points

The first pair are Lung 7 (Lu-7) and Kidney 6 (K-6), used for treating the lungs when they are under attack from a common cold. Lu-7 is massaged up the arm against the direction of the flow of chi in the lung meridian, to fight lung pathogens. K-6 is massaged up the leg in the direction of the flow of chi in the kidney meridian, to increase the power of the kidneys to support the lungs.

Triple Warmer 5 (TW-5) and Gall Bladder 41 (GB-41) are used to clear heat from the whole body in cases of high fever. TW-5 is massaged down the forearm against the direction of the flow of chi in the triple warmer meridian. GB-41 is massaged up the foot against the direction of the flow of chi in the gall bladder meridian. These paired points might be used with Lu-7 and K-6 to lower a high temperature.

Pericardium 6 (P-6) and Spleen 4 (Sp-4) are used for treating heartburn and inflammation of the digestive system. P-6 is massaged up the inside of the wrist against the direction of the flow of chi in the pericardium meridian, to reduce the heat in the pericardium and inflammation in the middle body cavity, through which this meridian flows. Sp-4 is massaged down the inside of the foot against the direction of the flow of chi in the spleen meridian to reduce the inflammation in the stomach and heart, through which this meridian flows.

The fourth pair are Small Intestine 3 (SI-3) and Bladder 62 (B-62), used to clear pain and inflammation from the upper back, neck, and shoulders. SI-3 is massaged down the hand against the direction of the flow of chi in the small intestine meridian. B-62 is massaged up the ankle against the direction of the flow of chi in the bladder meridian.

These points work because the pathways of their meridians overlap in the area of the upper back, neck, and shoulders. They would be used, for example, to treat whiplash, in conjunction with other local points.

More Information

For information on **meridian pathways** see pages 36–55.

POINT PRESSING
The eight trigram acupuncture points, which fall into pairs, are very influential in regulating the body's chi flow. Consequently, acupressure massage can improve your general health.

 Lung 7 (L-7) is used to reduce the activity of pathogenic factors in the lungs in cases of colds and flu. It is paired with K-6.

 Triple Warmer 5 (TW-5) is used to reduce excessive heat in cases of high-grade fever. It is paired with GB-41.

 Pericardium 6 (P-6) is used to reduce digestive troubles and nausea, indigestion and heartburn. It is paired with SP-4.

Small Intestine 3 (SI-3) is used to reduce pain, inflammation and swelling in the upper back, neck and shoulders. It is paired with BL-62.

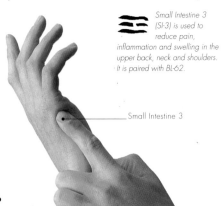

Small Intestine 3

 Kidney 6 (K-6) is used to reinforce the kidneys' chi to support the lungs, so that they can fight off pathogens. It is paired with L-7.

Bladder 62 (Bl-62) is used to reduce aching in the neck, shoulders and upper back. It is paired with SI-3.

Gall Bladder 41 (GB-41) is the point used to reduce excessive heat in the body. It is paired with TW-5.

Spleen 4 (SP-4) has the ability to reduce inflammation in the stomach and heart. It is paired with P-6.

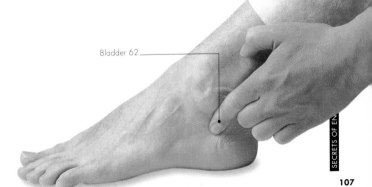

Bladder 62

Leading the Chi Through the Main Meridians

Meridian flow
Use the mind to regulate the chi.

Before carrying out this exercise, take a good look at the pictures of the meridian pathways on pages 38–55 and remember that it is necessary to lead the chi on both sides of the body simultaneously.

Exercise

Stand in The Mother Posture, with your eyes closed and your vision turned inwards. Lead the chi through the meridians with the power of your mind. Begin in the centre of the lower tan tien energy centre, in the middle of the lower belly. This is where the lung meridian begins. Lead the chi up into both lungs, then on to the neck, across the shoulders, and down the arms to the ends of the thumbs.

The chi now moves to the top of the index finger, which is the beginning of the large intestine meridian. Lead it up the arms and neck to the opposite sides of the nose, where it joins the stomach meridian. From here, lead it down the front of the torso, through the nipples, across the lower abdomen, and down the front of the thighs and shins to the end of the second toe.

The chi moves to the big toe, where it joins the spleen meridian. Lead the chi up the inside of the ankles, inner thighs, abdomen and chest to the front of the shoulders, where it joins the heart meridian. Lead it down the underside of the arms to the ends of the little fingers.

The chi now joins the small intestine meridian and rises up the back of both hands and arms, across the upper back, and up the neck to the eyes. It joins the bladder meridian, travels up the forehead, over the head, down both sides of the spine, through the buttocks and calf muscles, and along the outer foot to the end of the little toes. Here it joins the kidney meridian. Lead it under the feet and up the inside of the ankles and legs, through the groin and up the abdomen to the chest, where it joins the pericardium meridian. Let the chi travel down the inner arms and elbows to the end of the middle fingers.

Lead the chi to the triple warmer meridian through the ring fingers, up the backs of the hands, arms, shoulders neck, around the ears, and to the eyes.

More Information

For more information on **meridian pathways** see pages 38–55.

Awareness

Use your internal mind's eye to see the chi flow through the meridians.

LEADING THE CHI

After you have worked through pages 108–109, the gall bladder meridian becomes the focus. The chi zigzags over both sides of the skull, goes through the occipital cavity, down the sides of the torso and the outside of the legs, through the ankles and feet to the end of the fourth toe. Through the liver meridian, the chi rises up from the big toe over the top of the feet, up the inside of the legs, and through the groin. It then goes up the sides of the torso, into the liver, and back down into the lower tan tien energy centre. Gather and store the chi here.

Energy field

Practise chi kung by trees, where energy is strong.

Use the power of the
mind to lead the chi

Relaxed concentration
*Keep the mind focused and
concentrated, making sure that
there is no unnecessary mental
or physical tension.*

Keep the belly relaxed

Visualization
*Imagine your mind
leading the chi as a
thread tied to an arrow,
a ball of golden light
moving through a tunnel,
or as flowing water with
electric powers.*

The Small Circulation of Chi

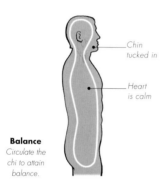

Chin tucked in

Heart is calm

Balance
Circulate the chi to attain balance.

The Small Circulation of Chi is practised while standing in The Mother Posture. We take the chi forwards from the lower tan tien energy centre to the front of the belly, then down the mid-line of the abdomen, under the torso, up through the governing meridian, over the top of the head, down the conception meridian, and back into the lower tan tien. This circular movement evenly distributes the energy between the back and front of the torso, the head, and belly. The governing and conception meridians are both able to store large amounts of chi, which is why they are sometimes called vessels rather than meridians. By circulating chi through them, we help to keep them full of chi. This is important so that they can act as reservoirs that the meridians in the rest of the body can draw upon. The governing meridian supplies all the yang meridians with chi, and the conception meridian supplies all the yin meridians.

Exercise

Smile towards the lower tan tien to programme your energy with a positive intention. Once the chi is activated, lead it through three, six, or nine circulations.

Bring the chi to Conception 4 (C-4) or C-6. Lead it down through the sexual organs, the perineum at C-1, the anus sphincter muscle, and Governing 1 (G-1) at the coccyx. Take the chi up the spine along points G-4, G-6, G-11, G-14, G-16 in the occipital cavity, and

G-20 on the top of the head. Then
move the chi to the third eye, between
the eyebrows. Lead it down through the
roof of the mouth, to the tip of the
tongue, and down the throat to C-22,
the chest to C-17, the solar plexus to C-
12, the navel to C-8, and finally back to
C-6 or C-4. To make more circuits,
simply move from C-6 or C-4 straight on
to the sexual organs and continue as
before. After completing three, six, or
nine orbits of The Small Circulation of
Chi, gather and store the chi in the
lower tan tien.

We can also move chi by breathing.
Inhale to take it up the back, and
exhale to allow it to flow back down
the front. Do not become dependent on
breathing for moving chi – it is more
important to use mental intention.

More Information

For information on **the third eye** see page 23.
For more information on **meridian pathways**
see pages 38–55.

Bask in chi
The warm glow of chi moving in the body feels just like the rays of the sun on the body.

SMALL CIRCULATION OF CHI The more
you practise, the greater the sensation of chi flow becomes. Eventually, chi will move through The Small Circulation with every breath you take, 24 hours a day. The more you practise, the greater the benefits that result – including improved health and a feeling of balance and well-being.

Tongue position
The tongue is placed on the roof of the mouth in the same position it would take if you said the letter 'L'.

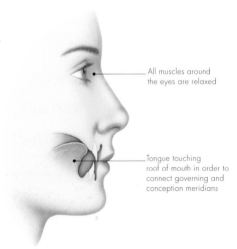

All muscles around the eyes are relaxed

Tongue touching roof of mouth in order to connect governing and conception meridians

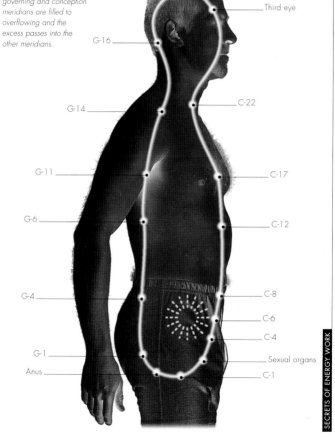

Filling the vessels
During this exercise, the governing and conception meridians are filled to overflowing and the excess passes into the other meridians.

G-20

Third eye

G-16

G-14

C-22

G-11

C-17

G-6

C-12

G-4

C-8

C-6

C-4

G-1

Sexual organs

Anus

C-1

The Earth to Heaven Flow of Chi

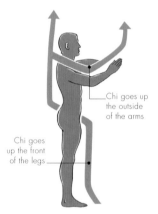

Chi goes up the outside of the arms

Chi goes up the front of the legs

Earth chi rising

Yin chi from the earth flows up to heaven.

The centre of the earth is full of yang fire, but the surface of the earth is very yin. Seventy per cent of the earth's surface is covered by water, which is yin. It is this cool blue, yin earth energy that flows up through us to heaven. (By heaven I mean the sun, moon, stars, and the cosmic forces of deep space.)

In this exercise we encourage chi to flow from earth to heaven through us. Chi kung breathing is not used – we just become aware of a natural chi flow through the body.

Exercise

Stand in The Mother Posture and imagine that there are roots of energy, like the roots of a tree, growing out of the acupuncture point Kidney 1 (K-1) on the soles of your feet. These roots spread wide and deep into the earth and it is through them that we draw up yin earth energy. The energy rises up through all the hard yang parts of the body, up over the big toes and the top of the feet, and then up the front of the legs. This may cause you to rock back ever so slightly.

The chi from each leg joins together at Conception 1 (C-1), the perineum, and travels up the spine to a point between the shoulder blades, where some of it branches off down the outside of the arms to the end of the fingertips. From there it rises up into the sky. When chi leaves the fingertips, they feel as though electricity is dancing through them.

The rest of the earth chi carries on up the spine and then up the back of the head. It leaves the body from Governing 20 (G-20) and ascends to heaven. This movement of chi, through G-20, feels like sparks on the top of the head.

Calming effect

The cool, blue healing chi of the earth, which is constantly rising up through our bodies, has a healing effect on all the internal organs. It also has a calming effect on an overheated, troubled mind, and soothes the emotions.

More Information

For more information on **The Earth to Heaven Flow of Chi** see pages 118–119.

Earth medicine
*The earth is a great
source of healing energy.*

EARTH TO HEAVEN FLOW OF CHI

When you have a strong connection with the earth, it is not only possible to feel its cool, healing chi rising up into you, but you may also be aware of any excess heat in your own system being released into the ground. This dispersal of heat means that mental restlessness and emotional irritability are reduced, and it becomes easier to attain the Wu Chi state.

TAO TE CHING

*Man follows earth
Earth follows heaven
Heaven follows tao
Tao follows itself*

LAO TZU

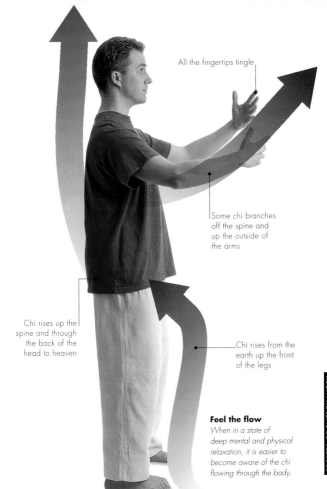

All the fingertips tingle

Some chi branches
off the spine and
up the outside of
the arms

Chi rises up the
spine and through
the back of the
head to heaven

Chi rises from the
earth up the front
of the legs

Feel the flow

*When in a state of
deep mental and physical
relaxation, it is easier to
become aware of the chi
flowing through the body.*

The Heaven to Earth Flow of Chi

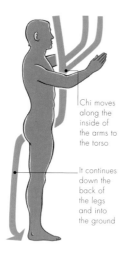

Chi moves along the inside of the arms to the torso

It continues down the back of the legs and into the ground

Heaven chi descending

Chi flows from the sky down through us.

In this exercise we learn to draw chi energy from heaven, through us, to the earth. No special chi kung breathing is used; we just become aware of natural chi flow.

Exercise

Stand in The Mother Posture and imagine that there are roots of energy, like the roots of a tree, growing out of the acupuncture point Kidney 1 (K-1) on the soles of your feet. Now visualize the sun shining down on you. Feel its warm glow bathing your face and palms. This golden, glowing energy is sparkling like starlight, as it descends into us through the acupuncture point Governing 20 (G-20) and through the tips of the fingers.

When the chi arrives at G-20, it feels like a dancing electric light on the top of the head. When the chi flows into the fingertips, they feel as though they are buzzing with electricity as well.

The chi flows down through all the yin, soft parts of the body. It travels along the inside of the arms and reaches the chest, from where it moves down the conception meridian. From G-20 it travels down the face and the front of the torso to the perineum at

Conception 1 (C-1), where it splits and moves down the back of the legs. This movement may cause you to rock forwards ever so slightly.

The chi then heads for the bottom of the feet, where it goes to K-1, and from there it enters the earth through the wide and deep tree-like energy roots that we visualized at the beginning of the exercise.

The chi energy coming from heaven is comprised of physical energies such as cosmic rays, solar rays, starlight, and the light of the sun that is reflected off the moon. Heavenly energy also contains energy that comes from the spirit world. These combined energies can have a powerful effect – not only on our body, but also on our mind and emotions.

More Information

For more information on **The Heaven to Earth Flow of Chi** see pages 122–123.

Heavenly healing
*We can be healed by
the power of heavenly chi.*

HEAVEN TO EARTH FLOW OF CHI

The previous exercise on Earth to Heaven chi flow (see page 116), and the opposite exercise of heaven to earth chi flow, are equally important for balancing and healing our body. When healing someone else, we use both the heaven and earth chi flowing through us to heal them.

OPEN SKY

Sky and earth are ageless,

Renewed by the breath of tao,

*If we cultivate this life
source and circulate it in
the body we can*

*be one with the
immortal earth and sky.*

THE IMMORTAL TAOIST

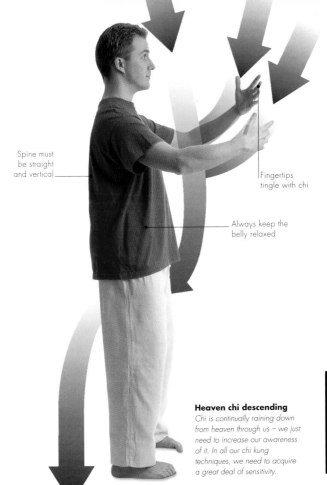

Spine must
be straight
and vertical

Fingertips
tingle with chi

Always keep the
belly relaxed

Heaven chi descending

*Chi is continually raining down
from heaven through us – we just
need to increase our awareness
of it. In all our chi kung
techniques, we need to acquire
a great deal of sensitivity.*

The Big Circulation of Chi

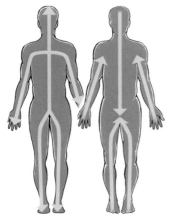

Major chi
*Heaven and earth chi
circulate together within us.*

The Big Circulation of Chi is an energy technique that unites both The Earth to Heaven Flow of Chi and The Heaven to Earth Flow of Chi exercises. This beneficial chi kung exercise balances the yin and yang chi in the body, at the same time as incorporating heaven and earth chi into the body.

The Big Circulation of Chi is the same as The Small Circulation of Chi, but also includes the arms and legs. It can be achieved through the power of the mind, with or without using special chi kung breathing.

Exercise

Stand in The Mother Posture and imagine that there are roots of energy, like the roots of a tree, growing out of the acupuncture point Kidney 1 (K-1) on the soles of the feet. These roots penetrate far and wide into the earth.

As you inhale, smile in the direction of the lower tan tien. As you exhale, lead the chi forwards to Conception 4 (C-4) or Conception 6 (C-6), then down through the sexual organs to the perineum at C-1. Here the chi splits and travels down the back of both legs. This may cause you to rock forwards a fraction. The chi then goes down to K-1 and into the ground through the roots previously visualized. Inhale and draw earth chi through the roots, over the big toes, along the top of the feet, then up

124

the front of the legs. This may make you rock backwards slightly. The chi from each leg joins at C-1 and travels up the spine to Governing 11 (G-11), between the shoulder blades.

Exhale, and let the chi branch off down the outside of the arms to the ends of the fingertips.

Inhale and bring the chi up the inside of the arms and across the back, where it meets at G-11, travels up the spine, over the head through G-20, and to the third eye, between the eyebrows.

Exhale and lead the chi down through the roof of the mouth to the tip of the tongue, down to the throat, C-22, the chest, C-17, the solar plexus, C-12, the navel, C-8, and finally back to C-6 or C-4.

After completing three, six, or nine orbits of The Big Circulation of Chi, gather and store the chi in the lower tan tien.

More Information

For information on **The Small Circulation of Chi** see pages 112–115.

Plug into the planet
We feel more in tune with nature when we are aware of our own natural chi flow.

BIG CIRCULATION OF CHI
In nature, the sun heats the sea and causes water to evaporate, rise upwards and become clouds. The clouds produce rain, which falls on to the mountains and flows into the sea where it is heated again. This natural cycle reflects the transformation of energy as it flows through The Big Circulation of Chi.

Practising The Big Circulation of Chi
This diagram shows the direction of chi flow during this exercise. We stand in The Mother Posture when we practise the exercise, and we can use breathing to help us, or just harness the power of the mind to lead the chi.

BIG CIRCULATION

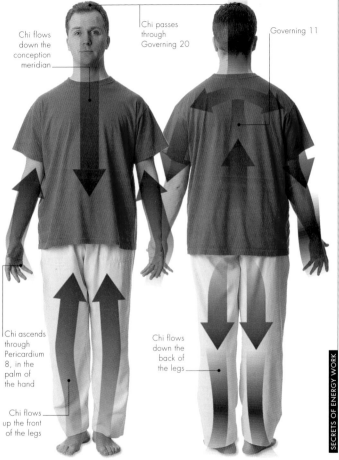

Chi passes through Governing 20

Chi flows down the conception meridian

Governing 11

Chi ascends through Pericardium 8, in the palm of the hand

Chi flows up the front of the legs

Chi flows down the back of the legs

The Thrusting Meridian and the Three Tan Tiens

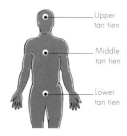

- Upper tan tien
- Middle tan tien
- Lower tan tien

Energy fields
The tan tiens lie on the thrusting meridian.

Imagine a line from Conception 1 (C-1) up to Governing 20 (G-20). This is the thrusting meridian, along which lie the tan tiens. The lower is connected with doing, the middle with feeling, and the upper with thinking. When they are in balance, thoughts, feelings and actions can be integrated.

Exercise

Stand in the Mother Posture and concentrate on the centre of the lower belly. The lower tan tien is located on the thrusting channel behind Conception 6 (C-6). It is the body's physical centre of gravity and is important for physical, mental, and emotional balance. When our actions and movements stem from here, they are more likely to be steady and balanced. This is the centre associated with decisive action, which is why it is emphasized in the practice of tai chi.

Now let the chi rise up the thrusting meridian to the middle tan tien. This is behind Conception 12, and is associated with our emotions. When our emotions trigger feelings of heartache and butterflies in the solar plexus, these are actually best controlled by strengthening the lower tan tien, which is associated with water and will calm and cool the heart fire of the middle tan tien.

The tan tiens are visualized as glowing, golden balls of light. The upper tan tien is in the centre of the head behind the third eye, between the eyebrows. When this tan tien is activated you will feel pressure in the occipital cavity. This is where spiritual knowledge enters and travels straight to our subconscious. You will also feel a spark of electricity in the third eye. The Chinese call this point The Gateway to the Spirit, and in acupuncture it is used to calm a restless mind. You will also experience a sensation of electric lights dancing on the top of the head. This gateway is not only where energy can enter and leave the body, but is also the main exit route for spiritual travelling.

When the upper tan tien is activated, our mental capacity and creativity is increased and our potential for spiritual development enhanced. At the end of the exercise, bring the chi down to the lower tan tien and store it there.

More Information

For information on **spirit travelling** see pages 206–215.

Worldly wise
Chi kung helps us to be calm in a stressful world.

THE THRUSTING MERIDIAN Lying in the

centre of the body, the thrusting meridian is the location for the three tan tiens. When these are all activated, one experiences a state of complete internal stillness, provided that the spine is kept straight and vertical.

TSAN-TUNG-CHI

Nourish yourself internally
In peace, stillness and emptiness,
Illuminate the entire body.
Look for it and
you cannot see it
Yet it is close by and
easy to get.

WEI PO-YANG

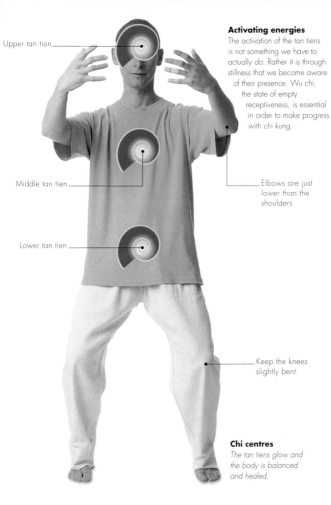

Middle tan tien

Lower tan tien

The activation of the tan tiens
is not something we have to
actually *do*. Rather it is through
stillness that we become aware
of their presence. Wu chi,
the state of empty
receptiveness, is essential
in order to make progress
with chi kung.

Elbows are just
lower than the
shoulders

Keep the knees
slightly bent

Chi centres

*The tan tiens glow and
the body is balanced
and healed.*

Exercises **The Thrusting Meridian**

SECRETS OF ENERGY WORK

The Chakra System

Chakras
*Yoga practice incorporates an
awareness of the chakras.*

There is another set of energy
centres on the thrusting meridian,
which are known as the seven
chakras. To activate each chakra one
by one, we can lead chi up through the
thrusting meridian. The experience of
moving through the chakras is like
becoming familiar with a rainbow of
colours, from infrared to ultraviolet and
white light. Use your internal mind's eye
to visualize the explosion of colour set
in motion by activation of the chakras.

The chakra system is associated with
Hindu yoga practitioners in India, but it
is also part of Buddhist teaching in
India, China and Southeast Asia.
Taoists in China give more emphasis to
the internal organs and tan tiens.

Exercise
Stand in The Mother Posture and
concentrate on acupuncture point
Conception 1 (C-1), located in the
perineum. Imagine a vertical line
through the centre of the body up to
Governing 20 (G-20) on the top of the
head. This is the thrusting meridian,
along which the seven chakras are
located. Guide your chi up the thrusting
meridian to each chakra, visualizing the
relevant colour as you do so.

When you have finished, bring the
chi back down the conception meridian
and store it in the lower tan tien.

More Information

For more information on **Governing and
Conception meridian points** see page 115.

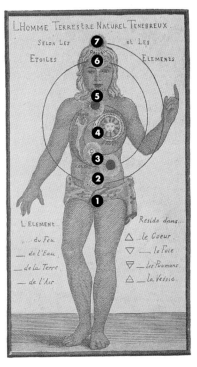

7 The seventh is located on G-20, and is visualized as a white ball of light. This is where all the colours unite and become white.

6 The sixth is located between G-16 and the third eye; it is seen as a purple ball of light.

5 The fifth is located between G-14 and C-22, and is visualized as a blue ball of light glowing in the centre of the throat.

4 The fourth is located between G-11 and C-17; it is a green ball of light.

3 The third is located between G-6 and C-12, and manifests as a yellow ball of light.

2 The second is located between G-4 and C-8; it is an orange ball of light.

1 The first is located at C-1, and is usually visualized as a red ball of light.

The magnificent seven
The chakras are represented by glowing balls of light.

ACQUIRED AND SEXUAL ENERGY

There are many chi kung techniques that make use of the body's sexual energy to improve health and creative power. Before these can be explained, we need to discuss what is meant by sexual energy. Sexual energy is considered to be a creative force within each individual, which usually peaks and falls in accordance with age. It governs a person's health, not just the ability to reproduce. ⟡ By incorporating sexual energy into our practice of chi kung, we can improve our health and change the course of our lives, possibly extending the length of time we live by many years. ⟡ The final spreads in this chapter deal with energy derived from food, or "acquired energy".

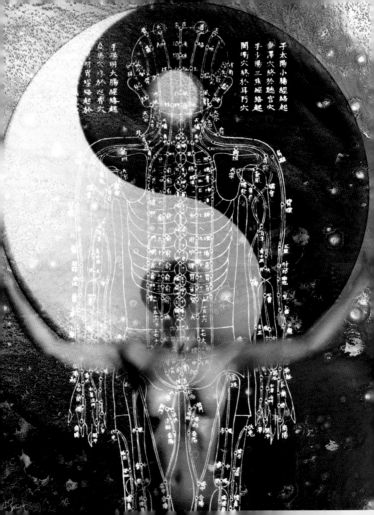

Chi Kung and Sex

Sexual energy is partly the genetic force inherited from our parents, and it is also a powerful force contained within our own kidneys.

Sexual energy is replenished by the energy from the food we eat and the air we breathe: acquired chi. Inherited chi, kidney chi, and acquired chi combine to form sexual energy.

Sexual energy also has some functions additional to reproduction. It can be taken from the sexual organs and redistributed around the body to improve health, and it can help a person be more creative.

Chi kung teaches that you should, as much as possible, conserve sexual energy unless it is being employed for reproductive purposes, so we do not exhaust our inherited chi and kidney chi too quickly. This allows us to stay powerful and strong well into old age.

The practice of Cool Sexual Energy Techniques and Hot Sexual Energy Techniques enable you to incorporate

Power of love
Love creates healing energy.

sexual chi into your overall energy system (see pages 140–145). These exercises will help you to maintain sexual potency and good general health longer than is normally considered possible, and will also steer you to achieve other life objectives thanks to the availability of more energy.

Seven yin and eight yang

The ancient Chinese associated the number 7 with seven-year periods in the sexual development and health of a woman (although there are variations due to genetic inheritance and environmental factors). The use of the number 7 in chi kung is known as "spiritual yin". The seven-year periods of woman are delineated as follows.

At the age of 7 her teeth and hair grow. At 14 she begins to menstruate and can bear children. At 21 she is fully grown and her physical condition is at its best. At 28 her muscles are firm and her body is flourishing. At 35 her face begins to wrinkle and her hair begins to fall. At 42 her arteries start to harden and her hair turns white. At 49 menstruation ceases and she can no longer have children.

The number 8 performs the same role in a man's life, and is called "spiritual yang". The eight-year periods of man are described as follows.

At the age of 8 his hair grows long and second teeth grow. At 16 he begins to secrete semen. At 24 his testicles are fully developed and he has reached his full height. At 32 his muscles are firm. At 40 his testicles begin to weaken, he begins to lose his hair, and his teeth begin to decay. At 48 his masculine vigour is exhausted, his face wrinkles, and his hair turns grey. At 56 his secretions diminish and his testicles deteriorate.

More Information

For more information on **chi kung and sex** see pages 138–145.

Buy me
Sex is used as a sales device by the advertising industry for everything. From cars to clothes, coffee to chocolate, sex sells.

CHI KUNG AND SEX

In the chi kung way of thinking, sex is not an external event that we are drawn towards; instead, it is an internal energy source that we can cultivate. When sexual energy is aroused, it causes blood flow to increase in the area of the sexual organs. Chi spreads from these organs and begins to affect the rest of the body. Blood circulation is invigorated and the skin becomes flushed. The nervous system is activated, even the optic nerve is affected, causing the pupils to dilate. Hormones are mobilized and rush around the body. It is evident that sexual energy can galvanize the whole body into being more active.

Desire
Acquiring mental control over sexual chi will stop your life being ruled by desire.

Judgement

*Sex is not good or bad, or right or wrong.
It is a natural force that flows in all of us.*

Body beautiful

*The chi shining out
from within reveals
itself in a glowing,
radiant body.*

Control

Sexual energy is such a
powerful force that it can
lead to acts of romantic
heroism and beautiful works
of art. Or, when suppressed
or denied, it can lead to
great savagery and
violence. So, developing
control of one's sexual
energy is vitally important.

Cool Sexual Energy Techniques

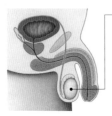

The Chinese refer to the testicles as the external kidneys

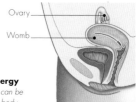

Ovary

Womb

Powerhouses of energy
Controlled sexual energy can be directed to energize the body.

When a person is excited, sexual energy is ready to expand. If we let it follow the usual route, it will go down and out of the body. In chi kung training we encourage sexual energy to expand up and into the body, to energize and strengthen it. It needs to be redirected into the meridian system, and pumped up into the body.

Before we attempt to control and channel sexual energy when it is in an excited, hot state of arousal, we should first practise making use of it while it is cool and calm. Hot sexual energy has much greater power and momentum than cool sexual energy, and is much

harder to control and direct. The closer a person gets to a climax, the less able he is to control his sexual energy. Therefore we first practise the techniques when sexual chi is cool, in the absence of sexual thoughts or activities. Then we practise when we are becoming aroused. Managing sexual chi in stages makes it easier to control when it is hot and forceful.

Spiritual Seven and Eight

It is possible to improve your health through other chi kung exercises without practising sexual chi kung methods. However, the concepts of The Spiritual Seven Yin and The Spiritual Eight Yang teach that sexual chi and general health are interconnected, and that at a certain age we reach a peak, after which our health begins to decline. For women, The Spiritual Seven Yin states that at 28 her body is flourishing; at 35 her health begins to decline.

Therefore, ideally, women should have begun learning the sexual chi kung methods by the time they are 28, and be practising them regularly by the time they are 35.

For men, The Spiritual Eight Yang states that at 32 his muscles are firm, while at 40 his testicles, hair and teeth begin to weaken.

So men should have begun learning the sexual chi kung methods by the time they are 32, and be practising them regularly by the time they are 40.

More Information

For more information on **Seven Yin and Eight Yang** see pages 136–137.

COOL SEXUAL ENERGY

For this technique we concentrate on an area called the pelvic floor. If it is exercised and kept toned and strong, we are less likely to develop problems relating to weakness of the genito-urinary system. The pumping action generated by the contractions of the exercise, synchronized with breathing, help to mobilize blood flow as well as chi flow, which is good for the general health of the whole body.

Breathing should be synchronized with pelvic contractions

The combination of breathing and steady pelvic contractions will help the chi to flow around your body

Moderation
Women should not practise these exercises during menstruation, and both men and women should only practise a little every day. Overworking this area would weaken it. A long-term improvement is achieved by sticking to a short period of regular daily training.

Chi travels up governing meridian

First exercise

Stand in The Mother Posture. As you inhale, pull in the lower abdomen and pull the sexual organs inwards and upwards as you lead the chi up the governing meridian to the top of the head. The internal muscles that pull up the sexual organs are the same ones that are capable of halting the flow of urine while urinating. As you exhale, allow the belly and sexual organs to relax and let the chi flow down the conception meridian to the lower tan tien energy centre.

Second exercise

The second exercise is exactly the same as the first, except that, on the inhalation, you pull the anal sphincter muscle up and in.

Third exercise

The third exercise is exactly the same as the first, except that when you inhale, you pull the perineum (the area between the sexual organs and the anus) up and in. (It is also good to practise a fourth exercise that pulls all three areas, the sexual organs, the anus, and the perineum, inwards and upwards at the same time.) When you have finished the exercise lead the chi down the conception meridian and gather and store it in the lower tan tien.

Hot Sexual Energy Techniques

Passion
Hot sexual chi kung for people in love.

Hot Sexual Energy Techniques are used during sexual intercourse. If both partners use them they will work more effectively, although one partner can practise without the other.

Controlling the energy

This energy is harder to control because it is excited. It is best to draw the energy up into the body before getting 50 per cent of the way to orgasm, because as the hot sexual energy gets close to its climax point it is very, very hard to restrain and direct.

The first thing you need to master is the contraction of the sexual organs, perineum and the anus – which is a closing and locking feeling, like closing a gate – rather than a sensation of pulling upwards. This is to make sure that the chi does not go down and out of the body. Once the "lower gate" has been closed you can pull upwards and inwards, synchronized with your breathing, and pump the chi up the spine and into the head. The area of the sexual organs will then feel empty while the head will feel full.

Press the tongue on to the roof of the mouth, relax the belly, and allow the head to empty and the lower tan tien to fill up with chi. Now you can release the lock on the lower gate. Next, re-arouse your sexual energy and repeat the exercise once more.

When you have finished, bring the chi back down the conception meridian and gather and store it in the lower tan tien. If you do not, the hot chi will overheat your brain and heart which could cause restlessness, insomnia, hyperaphrodisia, and headaches.

Whether or not a man should allow the sexual energy to get to 100 per cent and cause seminal emission depends, from a chi kung perspective, on his age and health. For a young man in good health it is fine; however, for an older man in poor health the loss of essence and chi would not be beneficial. In chi kung teaching it is believed that excessive loss of seminal essence can lead to a decline in health or an increase in the deterioration of the body associated with ageing.

More Information

For more information on **men's health** see page 137.

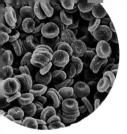

Healthy blood
The food we eat is used to make the blood, which nourishes the whole body.

ENERGY ASPECTS OF FOOD

In previous chapters we have explored how to obtain energy from air, earth, heaven, and from the various tan tien energy centres and meridians. However, there is one energy source that we are all dependent upon, whether we practise chi kung or not: the food we eat. Food energy is known as acquired chi and provides the nutrients we need to make blood and essence, and create the energy for the maintenance and defence of the body. If our blood, essence, and chi are nourished then our muscles, bones, and internal organs will be strong and our health good.

Summer
In the summer we need to eat lots of fruit and vegetables to help keep the body hydrated.

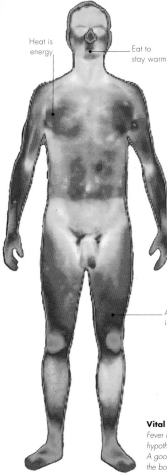

Heat is energy

Eat to stay warm

A warm body is a healthy body

Winter
In the winter we need to eat enough hot cooked food to enable us to fight the cold and maintain our core temperature.

Vital heat
Fever is excess heat, while hypothermia is deficient heat. A good healthy diet will keep the body warm and balanced.

The Energy Aspects of Food

Snack attack
One problem with the Western diet is our fondness for pre-prepared foods.

Another factor to consider in respect of food and drink is the various undesirable additives in our food today. It is best to buy fresh, organic food, rather than tinned or packaged foods that contain artificial flavours, colours, and preservatives. Fresh food contains more chi.

For those who eat meat, it is advisable to eat organically raised animals rather than those that are factory farmed and fed questionable foodstuffs. In my opinion, the best source of animal protein is white-fleshed fish such as cod, plaice, sole, halibut, and sea bass. These are very nutritious, easy to digest, and nourish the body's organs, muscles, tendons, sinuses, bones and senses.

Climate and food

When the winter weather is bitingly cold, our bodies burn up extra energy just trying to maintain the correct temperature. It is necessary not only to increase the amount we eat but also to have more hot, cooked food. During the hot summer months we should eat more fruit and vegetables and drink plenty of water to avoid dehydration.

Whatever the season, it is generally accepted that unusually low or high body temperatures are signs of illness. So it is very important to try to regulate body temperature as much as possible in order to maintain good health. We do this by dressing warmly in the winter and staying in the shade in summer. The same principle applies to what we eat and drink. Cold foods and drinks lower body temperature and should be avoided. The digestion of food is a warm process; this means the body heats the food up to break it down. So avoid ice-cream, chilled drinks and all cold foods because they will weaken the digestive system and its ability to extract nutrients from food.

The great debate about whether it is good or bad, right or wrong to be a meat eater or a vegetarian all depends on people's health and the climate they live in. For example, if Eskimos in the North Pole were vegetarians, they would die from hypothermia. Only a diet rich in animal protein can enable them to counter the cold. If a girl with serious anaemia decided to become a vegan she would find her health going into decline very rapidly. However, a vegetarian diet would be perfectly suitable for a healthy young person in a warm, tropical environment.

THE BONES

Bone is 30 per cent water, flexible, incredibly strong, and can withstand great amounts of pressure and stress. Bones grow and change as we grow. A baby has 350 bones, which grow together to become 206 bones by adulthood. The skeleton does not finish growing until we are about 25 years old. Bones need activity to maintain their density; they deteriorate with inactivity. Studies on astronauts, who lose bone density when they spend a long time in the weightless environment of zero gravity, confirm this. Chi kung and tai chi exercises relax the muscles and strengthen bone composition as well as helping bones to regenerate marrow to improve blood production. The flesh becomes a weight we carry with the bones rather than hold up with the muscles. This pressure and weight on bones help them to maintain density.

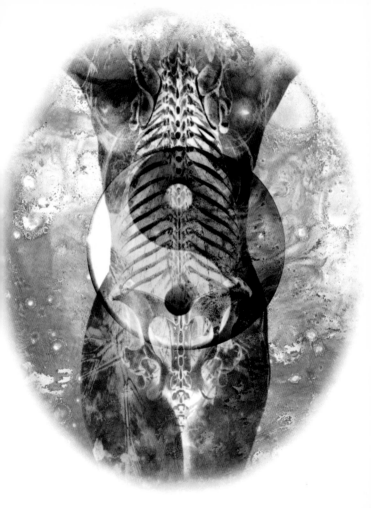

Improving Bone Health

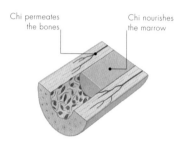

Chi permeates the bones

Chi nourishes the marrow

"Tiger's bones"
Chi kung strengthens bone structure and density.

The following techniques are designed to improve the health of the bones. However, because the body is a single integrated unit, there are many other benefits. The immune system is interconnected with the blood, and blood production is dependent on healthy marrow in the bones. Our immune system recognizes and destroys anything foreign to the body, including bacteria and toxic compounds. This recognition and destruction is performed by cells in the circulatory and lymphatic systems that are produced in the bone marrow.

The exercises for the spine will have a beneficial effect on the whole nervous system, because every nerve in the body begins in the spine.

Through chi kung training your awareness of your bones will increase and you will feel their density and power strongly: a quality particularly sought after by martial artists, who refer to having "tiger's bones".

Use these techniques to gain dense, flexible bones and to avoid brittle bone disease and osteoporosis. When an old person who has not strengthened her bones falls over, she is likely to fracture or break a bone. This can result in surgery, with all its possible complications, and mobility is often restricted afterwards. Therefore, it is important to build up the power of the bones so that they maintain the strength of their youth well into old age.

More Information

For more information on **women's health** see pages 136–7.

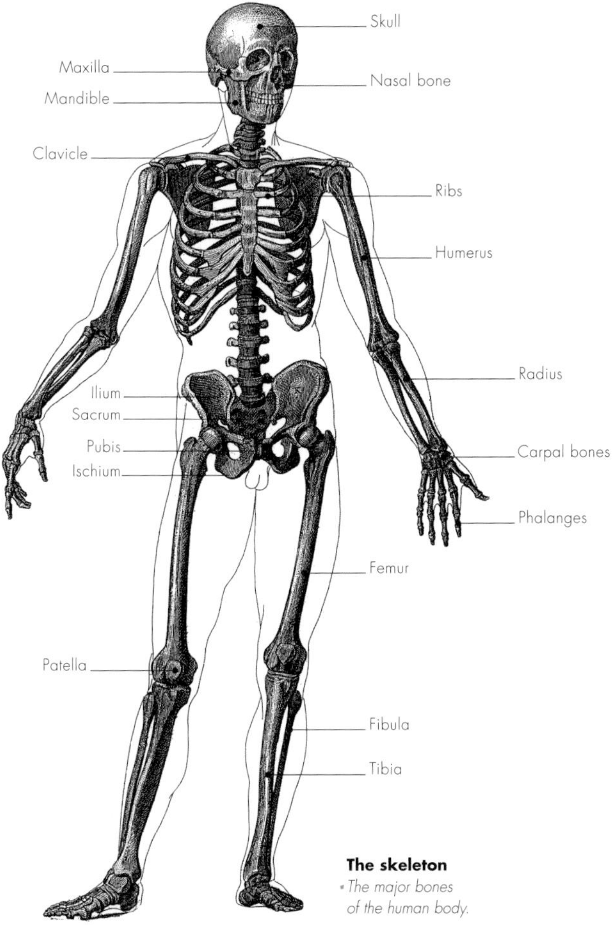

Skull

Maxilla

Mandible

Nasal bone

Clavicle

Ribs

Humerus

Radius

Ilium

Sacrum

Pubis

Ischium

Carpal bones

Phalanges

Femur

Patella

Fibula

Tibia

The skeleton

* The major bones
of the human body.

KIDNEY BREATHING

According to the principles of chi kung, the health of the bones is controlled by the kidneys. Before we begin to work directly on the bones, we need to strengthen the kidneys. We do this by breathing with them. The feeling is exactly the same as breathing with the lungs, except that it is chi, not air, that causes the expansion and contraction of the kidneys.

1 Energize the hands
Begin by standing in The Son Posture and practising Charging Up the Hands for Healing. Lean forwards slightly and place the acupuncture point Pericardium 8 (P-8), in the palms of the hands, over Bladder 23 (B-23), which is right on top of the kidneys.

Pericardium 8

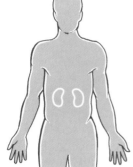

Kidney strength
Healthy kidneys regulate bone structure and density.

Pericardium 8
covers Bladder 23

Lean forwards
slightly

Kidneys become
warm and full

2 Hold the kidneys
*It now feels like the kidneys
are nestled in the palms of the
hands, which are full of warm
healing energy.*

3 Heal the kidneys
*To breathe with the kidneys,
inhale and feel them expand,
pressing on to the palms. As you
exhale, let the chi in the hands
flow out of P-8 into the kidneys.
Continue breathing in the same
way until the hands feel empty
and the kidneys feel warm and
full. Practising this particular
chi kung method, before you
undertake other bone-healing
exercises, will greatly increase
their effectiveness.*

Bone Breathing with the Hands

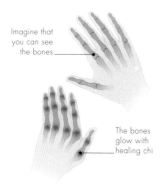

Imagine that you can see the bones

The bones glow with healing chi

Healing hands
We can counter wear and tear on the hands with chi kung.

When we use the word "breathing" for anywhere but the lungs, it means expanding and contracting the chi in that part of the body. This chi kung idea is called "bone breathing" when it is applied to any part of the skeletal structure of the body. The first bone breathing method we will look at is for the hands, because they probably undergo more wear and tear than any other part of the body. We concentrate on the hands not just because we don't want them to swell and become arthritic, but also because we are more familiar with them than any other part of our bodies – we see and use them almost every waking hour.

To be effective, this exercise requires that you have a good knowledge of all the little bones that make up the hand, so consult an anatomy book to get an idea of what they look like so that you have a realistic mental picture of them.

Exercise

Begin by standing in The Mother Posture, concentrating your awareness on your hands. Look at your hands and imagine that you can see through the skin to the bones. Visualize all the bones in the hands.

Once you are aware and concentrated on the hands, imagine a cloud of chi around them, like a warm glow of golden light. As you inhale, imagine the chi travelling out from the bones towards the skin surface and just outside the body. Then, as you exhale, imagine the chi rushing back into the bones. You should feel the bones being pressurized by the chi, as it needs to squeeze into the bones.

Continue bone breathing until the hands feel as heavy as lead. This is all accomplished with the power of the mind in coordination with the breathing. There is no tensing of the muscles involved as it would just block the chi flow. (Some people talk about hard and soft chi kung, but there is really only soft chi kung – any hardness in the body would block the flow of chi.) So, the key to success is having no unnecessary tension in the body.

More Information

For information on **relaxation** see pages 172–205.

BODY BONE BREATHING

Once you have mastered bone breathing with the hands, you can move on to bone breathing with the body. The idea now is to use all the bones in the skeletal structure. When you are doing this correctly, the whole skeletal structure starts to vibrate and every bone in your body buzzes, which is a very pleasant sensation. The compression of chi into the bones makes them denser and regenerates the marrow, a major part of the body's blood production system, so this exercise is good for general health and essential for those who are practising chi kung for longevity.

Breathing bones

1 *Stand in The Mother Posture and try to be aware of your skeleton. Imagine every bone in your body pulsing with golden light. Begin the bone breathing.*

2 *When you inhale, imagine the chi travelling from the bones to the skin's surface.*

3 *As you exhale, imagine the chi rushing back into all the bones.*

4 *Continue bone breathing until the entire skeleton feels heavy and buzzing.*

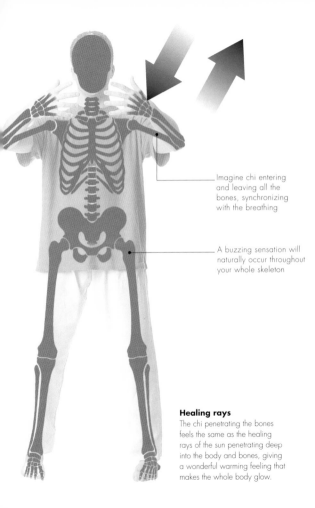

Imagine chi entering and leaving all the bones, synchronizing with the breathing

A buzzing sensation will naturally occur throughout your whole skeleton

Healing rays
The chi penetrating the bones feels the same as the healing rays of the sun penetrating deep into the body and bones, giving a wonderful warming feeling that makes the whole body glow.

Bone Breathing with the Joints

This technique involves both the bones and the connective tissue between them. It involves the expansion and contraction of the ligaments inside the joints in the body, in particular the ones in the upper body.

The expansion and contraction of the spaces between the bones generates chi in the joints, which can then be absorbed by the ends of the bones.

Tai chi practitioners work to develop explosive power in the whole body, first by cultivating their sinews and tendons. A person shot by an arrow suffers an injury caused by the power supplied to the arrow by the bowstring. It is the same with the body – it is not the fist that causes injury to the opponent but the power supplied to it by the elastic, resilient, expanding, contracting qualities of the tendons and ligaments.

In tai chi this power is cultivated while moving, and this exercise also develops it through attitude.

Arms like the branches

Body like the tree trunk

Bone stretching
The Tai Chi Fighting Stance is used for this chi kung exercise.

Exercise

This chi kung exercise is practised in the Tai Chi Fighting Stance. This is very similar to The Mother Posture, except that one foot is positioned a step in front

of the other, causing one hand to be
in front of the other. Let go of the arms
and hands and let them hang from the
spine, like the branches of a tree
hanging from the trunk. The main
work in this exercise is mental, rather
than the actual physical movement.
Let go of the tension inside the
shoulder joint, then inside the wrist,
and then in all the bones in the
hands, so that they lengthen and get
stretched by the weight of the bones
pulling them.

As you inhale, imagine the distance
between the bones inside the joints
lengthening. As you exhale, imagine
them contracting together. I must stress
that it is more of an internal feeling that
you are striving for, rather than an
external physical movement.

More Information

For more information on **tai chi** see pages 220–221.

STRAIGHTENING THE SPINE Most

people have an S-shaped spine. This is normal and healthy. However, to practise the next chi kung self-healing method of Bone Breathing with the Joints of the Spine, the spine must be kept straight and vertical.

Straightening out

1 Stand in The Mother Posture and concentrate on your spine. The coccyx should be tilted forwards to straighten the lower back. If you bend your knees, you will probably be putting it into the correct position.

2 Next, pull the chin in and lift the head up and back to straighten the upper back and neck. Imagine a string attached to the back of the top of your head, pulling upwards, and a weight attached to your lower back, pulling downwards and stretching the spine.

S-SHAPED SPINE

STRAIGHT SPINE

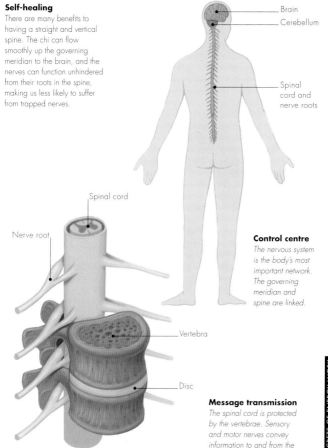

Self-healing

There are many benefits to having a straight and vertical spine. The chi can flow smoothly up the governing meridian to the brain, and the nerves can function unhindered from their roots in the spine, making us less likely to suffer from trapped nerves.

Brain

Cerebellum

Spinal cord and nerve roots

Spinal cord

Nerve root

Vertebra

Disc

Control centre

The nervous system is the body's most important network. The governing meridian and spine are linked.

Message transmission

The spinal cord is protected by the vertebrae. Sensory and motor nerves convey information to and from the central nervous system.

Bone Breathing with the Joints of the Spine

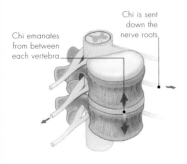

Chi emanates from between each vertebra

Chi is sent down the nerve roots

Power healer
The exercise generates a pulsewave of chi in the spine.

The chi kung practice of Bone Breathing with the Joints of the Spine is one of the most subtle to appreciate. Most people only have their attention drawn to their insides when they get a pain from an internal health problem, and then they get treatment to make it go away. Few people ever intentionally try and develop their internal vision to see and feel what is happening deep down inside themselves, or feel their chi more.

This book has so far provided you with a familiarity with the meridians, organs, energy centres, and, most recently, the bones. Now our chi kung is going to take us into the centre of the largest piece of bone in the body. We are going to generate a pulsewave of chi in the spine, from between each of the vertebrae, which is then sent down all the nerves that have their roots in the spine to heal the nervous system and all the internal organs that the nerves connect to and control.

This chi kung technique is a combination of bone breathing and joint breathing. It will enable the student to have great spinal flexibility, not the type of flexibility that lets you touch your toes, but an internal flexibility. With practice you will be able to reposition misaligned vertebrae individually from within your own body. Sensitivity and gentleness are necessary for this chi kung exercise.

TSAU TUNG-CHI

*As the chi flows the muscles
and skin glow.*

*The body's trunk is like
a tree with branches.*

*Concealed and hidden
to most people, it is unknown.*

Great virtue and chi are like gold.

WEI PO-YANG

More Information

For more information on spinal joint breathing
see pages 166–167.

SPINAL JOINT BREATHING

The disc and vertebrae couples of the spine are like positive- and negative-ended batteries. We can join them all up to form one big battery capable of releasing a very large charge. We do this by settling our lumbar vertebrae so that they all connect together. The spine must be straight, vertical, and internally connected.

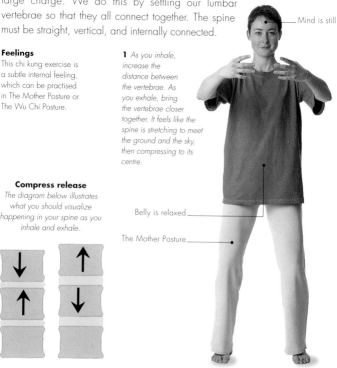

Mind is still

Feelings

This chi kung exercise is a subtle internal feeling, which can be practised in The Mother Posture or The Wu Chi Posture.

1 As you inhale, increase the distance between the vertebrae. As you exhale, bring the vertebrae closer together. It feels like the spine is stretching to meet the ground and the sky, then compressing to its centre.

Belly is relaxed

The Mother Posture

Compress release

The diagram below illustrates what you should visualize happening in your spine as you inhale and exhale.

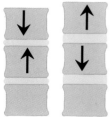

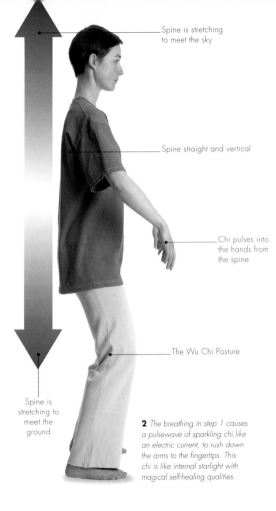

Spine is stretching
to meet the sky

Spine straight and vertical

Chi pulses into
the hands from
the spine

The Wu Chi Posture

Spine is
stretching
to meet the
ground

2 The breathing in step 1 causes
a pulsewave of sparkling chi, like
an electric current, to rush down
the arms to the fingertips. This
chi is like internal starlight with
magical self-healing qualities.

Opening and Closing the Kwa of the Spine

Kwa breathing
Opening and closing the spine and arm kwa.

The kwa can create such a powerful chi-pumping process that your chi expands and fills out the body like a balloon. Our defensive chi is expanded significantly as well, which helps us combat disease. Another benefit of opening and closing the kwa is that as the chi expands, it feels as though you are expanding beyond the confines of the physical body. It is sometimes possible to be able to look down and see the physical body doing the chi kung by itself (see pages 206–215). In this sense, kwa could also be interpreted as the bridge between this world and the spirit world.

The word "kwa" means "a semicircular bridge". A kwa is also sometimes referred to as a bow, like an archer's longbow. In this exercise, opening and closing refers to bending and straightening the two main kwa of the body in conjunction with chi kung breathing.

Exercise

The vertical spine kwa is a single line from the coccyx up the spine to the crown of the head. The horizontal arm kwa is a line from the tip of your middle finger, up the outside of the arm, across the back, and down the outside of the other arm to the tip of the other middle finger. It looks like a horizontal horseshoe shape. To perform the exercise, stand in The Mother Posture. To open the kwa, you must straighten them: keep the hands apart, the spine straight, and the breath and lower belly in. To close the kwa, bend them: put the hands together, curve the spine, keep the breath and lower belly out. Practise slowly and for at least five minutes.

When you have finished, gather and store the chi in the lower tan tien.

Opening and closing begins as a visible physical movement, but eventually becomes an internal movement of energy that we feel but cannot see. Opening and closing is breathing not just with the belly, but with the whole body.

More Information

For information on **breathing** see pages 68–71.

Fontanelles
A baby's skull is soft and open on the top, to enable it to move in order to pass through the birth canal when it is born.

SKULL BREATHING
We receive spiritual information through an area on the back of the head in the occipital cavity, but it usually goes straight into our subconscious and takes a lot of effort to access consciously. This exercise aims to open a point on top of the head, not physically but energetically, so that we can spiritually travel from there. A side-effect of Skull Breathing is that it energizes the brain, and can enhance imaginative and creative ability.

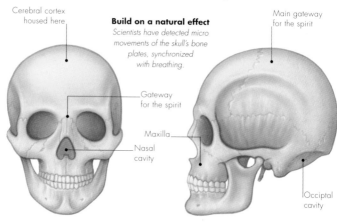

Cerebral cortex housed here

Build on a natural effect
Scientists have detected micro movements of the skull's bone plates, synchronized with breathing.

Main gateway for the spirit

Gateway for the spirit

Maxilla

Nasal cavity

Occiptal cavity

FRONT SKULL

SIDE SKULL

Do not overdo this exercise or it will cause the brain to overheat

As you inhale, visualize the skull expanding and filling with chi

1 *Stand in The Mother Posture and imagine the head is surrounded by a gentle glow of golden healing chi.*

2 *As you inhale, feel the sensation of the skull expanding and filling with chi. When you exhale, feel the skull returning to its original size.*

3 *Always bring chi back to the lower tan tien after this exercise.*

Chi Kung
Movement Sequences

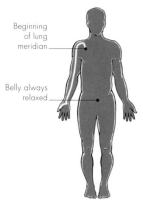

Beginning
of lung
meridian

Belly always
relaxed

Chi storehouse
The lung is the first of the 12 meridians.

All the chi kung exercises on the following pages (extending up to page 205) incorporate every one of the chi kung techniques that I have explained so far. All of these movements are completed by mental intention rather than muscle tension. We are being physically active without any unnecessary physical tension. This then paves the way for the ability to be mentally active without any unnecessary mental tension. Relaxation is a habit that many people need to relearn. "Trying" to relax creates tension. Instead you must "allow" yourself to relax. There should be no tension in the muscles, so there is no restriction to the flow of blood and chi. Where the chi goes the blood follows, so by increasing the chi flow we also increase the circulation of the blood, which has beneficial effects.

Before practising any of the sequences it is beneficial to stand in The Mother Posture for 15 minutes to release chi from the lower tan tien energy centre into the rest of the body.

Pleasant experiences

When practised correctly, there are many enjoyable sensations that one feels while performing the exercises. A sense of weightlessness is one feature, as if you are in zero gravity. There is an inner feeling like warm, electric, liquid mercury flowing through the body. You may feel as though you are swimming through the air as if it is water.

The movements of the body are totally integrated with breathing, which should be as long, slow, calm, and smooth as possible. Your breathing should be so quiet that even you cannot hear it. Keep your mouth closed and breathe through the nose. This breathing should not be forced, but allowed to happen by itself.

The cycle within this exercise is that the body follows the chi, the chi follows the mind, and the mind moves in harmony with nature.

Make sure that you stay centred in the lower tan tien and allow rotation of the belly to move the hands and feet.

More Information

For more information on **tai chi** see pages 220–221.

GRASPING THE SPARROW'S TAIL

This is a flowing sequence of chi kung movements, which balances and regulates the chi in the lung and large intestine meridians and organs. The whole sequence can be repeated – it is best to practise it at least nine times. Gather and store the chi in the lower tan tien after exercising.

1 *Stand with the right foot a comfortable step forwards, but retain all the other aspects of structure as The Mother Posture. This posture is called Double Peng. Seventy per cent of the weight is on the right leg.*

2 *Turn the hands over and move the belly and hips to the left as you bring the hands down. This is called Roll Back. Seventy per cent of the weight is now on the left leg.*

3 *This posture is called Squeeze. Place the left hand in the right. Move the hands forwards and up as you turn the waist to the right and transfer your weight so that seventy per cent of it is on the right leg.*

Darting sparrow
*The hands move like
the wings of a sparrow.*

6 *Fishes in Eight continues
by moving your weight
and waist to the right and
pointing the left hand to the
inside of the right elbow.*

4 *Sit back and open the
hands. Then bring the
weight forwards again.
This is called Press.*

5 *This move is
called Fishes in Eight.
Move your weight and
waist to the left and point
the right hand to the inside
of the left elbow.*

Waving Hands Like Clouds

Cloud Hands
The stomach meridian is healed by these movements.

This is a flowing sequence of chi kung movements, designed to balance the chi energy in the stomach and spleen meridians and organs, called Cloud Hands.

This sequence is particularly effective in developing an important chi kung principle called sung. The word "sung" describes the process of letting go of unnecessary tensions in the body and mind, and relaxing and sinking into the chi kung posture. Releasing physical tension makes it easier to disperse mental tension, which in turn enables us to let go of physical tension, and so on. In sung we are at ease and alert, calm and focused. A person's hand–eye coordination and response speed is improved when they are sung.

When the body is sung the mind can be sung; when the mind is sung the body can also be sung. When we are sung our bodies become more supple, elastic, and resilient. These youthful qualities can continue to be developed as we get older, so that we don't suffer from the ailments of old age.

You know you are in a state of sung if you do not feel your wrists moving as the hands change from yin to yang and back again. The yin–yang hand change is the same movement as that of the wings of a bird in flight.

BALANCE

If hard like dead wood,

wind blows, you break.

If soft like grass,

wind blows, you bent.

If like bamboo,

bend and spring back.

This is the way of yin and yang.

THE IMMORTAL TAOIST

More Information

For more information on **yin–yang hands** see pages 72 and 76.

WAVING HANDS LIKE CLOUDS

The whole sequence can be repeated again and again: continue slowly for at least five minutes. Gather and store the chi in the lower tan tien after exercising.

1 *Begin by standing in The Mother Posture, but with the right hand up and the left down. Turn the waist to the right, moving the weight on to the right leg slightly.*

2 *Turn the right hand palm down and move the hand down, while the left hand (palm up), moves upwards inside the right wrist.*

3 *Start to move the waist to the left as you transfer your weight on to the left leg.*

4 *Turn both hands over as you turn your waist to the left and move the weight further on to the left leg.*

An airy feeling
The wrists feel as light as clouds.

5 *With the left hand palm down, move the hand down, while the right hand, palm up, moves upwards inside the left wrist. To complete the movement, turn the waist to the right, moving your weight to the right leg, and repeat the sequence.*

Heals chi in spleen and stomach

Wrists are sung

Brush Knee and Twist Step

Balancing the heart
The heart meridian flows down the inside of the arms.

This sequence of chi kung movements is designed to balance the chi energy in the heart and small intestine meridians and organs. This particular sequence must be practised as slowly as possible. The heart and the emotional mind are connected, so to calm the heart and

mind and ease stress and restlessness, we move so slowly that we cannot feel the movements. If our movements are calm, smooth, and flowing, our chi will mirror this internally, streaming smoothly throughout our bodies, balancing and healing us, producing mental calm and a state of well-being. Also, by practising slowly, we can more easily enter into a deeper state of relaxation and the chi kung becomes a type of movement meditation.

The flow of yin and yang

With conventional exercise, such as running, cardiovascular pressure forces blood around the body. In contrast, these chi kung movements work by generating gentle centrifugal and centripetal forces, which encourage the energy and blood to flow from the centre of the torso out to the extremities and back again. This brings about an improvement in the circulation without straining the heart.

During this chi kung movement sequence the waist turns from side to side. This natural, fluid movement is both yin and yang. Yin is centripetal, spiralling inwards; yang is centrifugal, spiralling outwards. The forces that are generated create a flow through the body that causes the wrists to spiral yin inwards and yang outwards. An energetic connection can be felt between the lower tan tien and the diagnostic pulses of traditional Chinese medicine, located on the radial artery at the wrist.

All the movement of the torso must come from the rotation of the spine, which must be kept straight and vertical. Also, in order to ensure that the head moves with the body, the nose must be kept over the navel.

More Information

For more information on **the heart** see pages 40–42.

BRUSH KNEE AND TWIST STEP

For this exercise keep the centre of gravity low, and don't rise up as you move forwards. Keep the knees bent, as this will make the legs stronger. Keep the weight forwards as the palm strikes, then turn the toes out, with the weight on the front heel. Repeat 12 times, then store chi in the lower tan tien.

1 *Shape the hands as if holding a large ball. Turn the waist to the right so that the weight is completely on the right leg.*

2 *As you bring the right hand up, brush the left knee with the left hand.*

3 *Step forwards with the left foot and turn the waist to the left. Bring the right hand in front of you.*

4 Keep the weight forwards on the left leg as you turn the hips a little back to the right. Slightly drop the right elbow as you do a palm strike with the right hand.

5 The waist is now turned back to the left with the weight completely on the left leg. Shape the hands as if holding a large ball, right hand on top.

6 Bring the left hand up and brush the right knee with the right hand. Do the same movement on the other side.

Ankles are sung

Bending Backwards

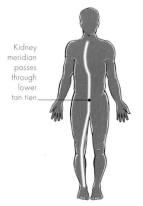

Kidney meridian passes through lower tan tien

Store of inherited energy
The kidneys control the bones and sexual energy.

There is a side-to-side aspect, as well as the backwards and forwards, to this movement. Therefore all the muscles around the belly get a workout. All of the chi kung movement sequence exercises provide general toning for the muscles, improve posture (both when still and moving), and develop better balance and coordination.

The spiralling and twisting movements of the torso and the subtle rotations of all the joints make the whole body flow like a great river. When chi kung is practised in this way we feel the energy spiralling up and down around the arms, legs, and torso.

All these sequences develop greater self-awareness and an increased sense of well-being. The stress release and relaxation response they create helps improve general health and encourages peace of mind.

When practising this exercise, begin very slowly and only arch the back very slightly, so there is a small compression. Don't hurry: slow progress always lasts longer than a quick fix.

The Bending Backwards sequence of chi kung movements is intended to balance chi energy in the kidney and bladder meridians and organs. It is the physical stretch, compression, and release of the kidneys in the lower back and the bladder in the lower belly, created by the movement, which heals them. Don't bend too much, though.

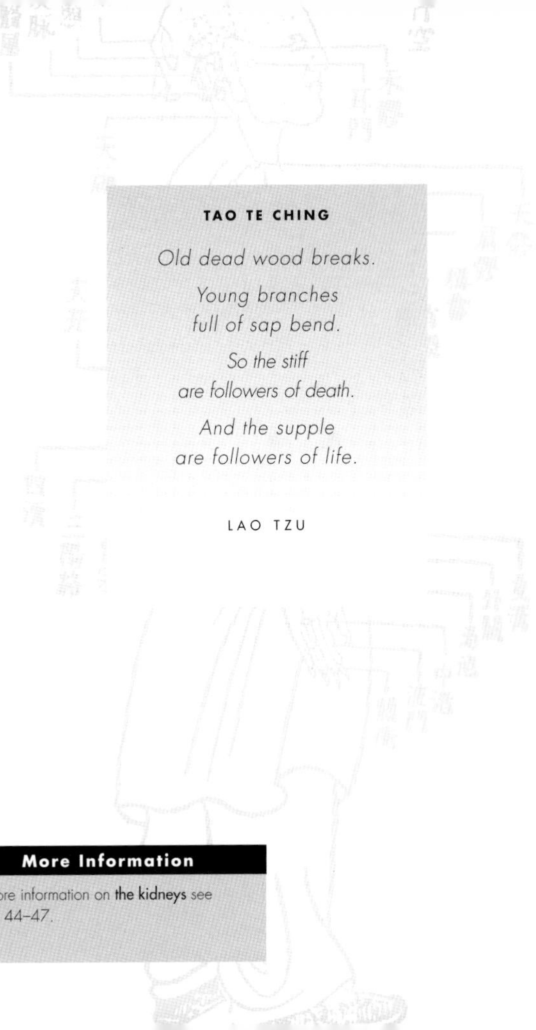

TAO TE CHING

Old dead wood breaks.

*Young branches
full of sap bend.*

*So the stiff
are followers of death.*

*And the supple
are followers of life.*

LAO TZU

More Information

For more information on **the kidneys** see
pages 44–47.

BENDING BACKWARDS

The feeling in the body created by this chi kung exercise is like that of throwing a lasso. The arms and spine also feel as flexible as thick rope, curved in both shape and movement.

1 Stand in The Mother Posture, but with the right foot a step forwards. Turn the waist to the right and place all the weight on the right leg. Hold the hands in relaxed fist shapes. Hold the right hand palm up by the right hip, while the left fist punches down.

2 Bring the left hand up to chest height and start to turn to the left, raising the right hand.

3 Turn the waist to the left and transfer the weight on to the left leg. Bring the right hand up in front of the face as you arch the lower back slightly.

Relaxed fist shape

4 With the weight still on the left leg, turn the hips to the right and move the right hand over the head.

5 Turn the waist back to the left and place the weight on the right leg. Turn the right hand palm upwards.

6 The weight is now forwards on the right leg. Curve the body forwards a little and start again. The whole sequence can be repeated two or three times. Gather and store the chi in the lower tan tien after exercising.

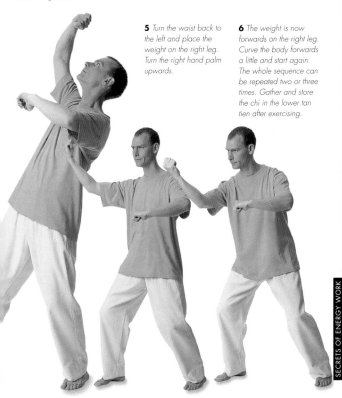

Opening the Gates

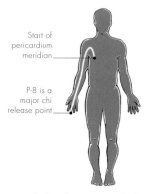

Start of pericardium meridian

P-8 is a major chi release point

Pericardium protects the heart

The pericardium meridian runs to the tip of the middle finger.

The aim of this sequence of chi kung movements is to balance the chi energy in the pericardium and triple warmer meridians. The pericardium is an organ that surrounds and protects the heart, but the triple warmer is not an actual organ, rather it is a process.

We have already learnt about the three body cavities – upper, middle, and lower. These cavities are known

as the three heating spaces or warmers. The upper body cavity contains the heat of respiration, the middle body cavity contains the heat of digestion, and the lower body cavity contains the heat of reproduction. The triple warmer meridian runs through all three of these body cavities and helps to regulate the temperature between these three different areas.

If there is excess heat trapped in the body, we need to clear it by acupuncturing Triple Warmer 5 and Gall Bladder 41, as well as Lung 7 and Kidney 6. Although acupuncture is the best method, acupressure should also help to alleviate this problem. Please refer to pages 104–107 for further details.

To gain a deeper understanding of tai chi and chi kung, I recommend the study of acupuncture.

More Information

For more information on **Pericardium 8 and the triple warmer** see pages 48–50.

TSAN TUNG CHI

*The mirror of the sun is the
yang fire that makes light.*

*If not for the moon and stars
how could we collect yin essence?*

*The yang sun and yin moon
are balanced fire and water
in the body.*

WEI PO-YANG

OPENING THE GATES

This exercise is usually practised at the beginning of a chi kung sequence, to open up all three body cavities to the flow of energy. As the chi is released, one feels a rushing sensation from the torso to the head.

1 *Begin by standing in The Wu Chi Posture. Circle the hands up and out as you rise up a little on the balls of the feet and inhale.*

2 *Bring the hands down and turn the feet out. Bend the knees and exhale.*

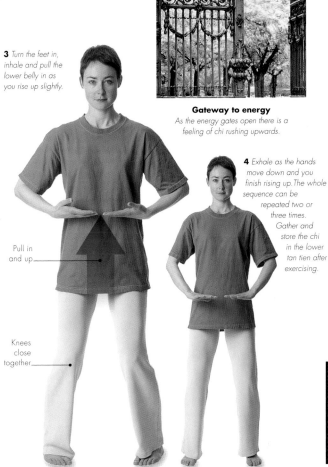

3 Turn the feet in, inhale and pull the lower belly in as you rise up slightly.

Gateway to energy
As the energy gates open there is a feeling of chi rushing upwards.

4 Exhale as the hands move down and you finish rising up. The whole sequence can be repeated two or three times. Gather and store the chi in the lower tan tien after exercising.

Pull in and up

Knees close together

Step Back and Repulse Monkey

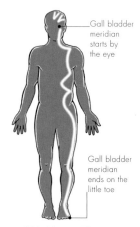

Gall bladder meridian starts by the eye

Gall bladder meridian ends on the little toe

Gall bladder meridian
The gall bladder meridian can be used to control the downwards movement of chi.

The liver and gall bladder meridians and organs benefit from this chi kung sequence, which is intended to balance their chi. The liver controls the tendons. All chi kung movement exercises are designed to develop a type of heavy, loose, relaxed, whole-body elastic power that comes from the tendons and sinews, rather than normal strength, which is derived from localized stiff muscle power. This elastic power is known as internal power.

To understand this phenomenon, consider the difference between an axeman chopping down a tree and a carpenter hammering in a single nail. The axeman uses his whole body in an integrated way, making use of his waist rotation and leg power as well as his arms in each of his cutting strokes. The carpenter, however, only uses his arm each time he strikes the nail, while the rest of his body moves very little.

With the development of internal power we gain a spring in our step and a noticeable vitality, so that as we get older we stay flexible and active. Inevitably, as a person acquires more chi and more internal power, his body resistance gets stronger, his overall vitality increases, and his chances for a longer life in good health improve. Another reason why it is important to balance and regulate the liver is because an internal branch of its meridian travels right up through the brain to the top of the head. If the liver is stressed, this causes mental restlessness and irritability. If this applies to you, practise the exercise very slowly in order to calm the liver.

Anger

If you find that you have bouts of anger, this may be due to the liver overheating. Make sure that you avoid spicy and deep-fried food and that you eat lots of fruit and vegetables. Chrysanthemum tea has a cooling effect, so drink cups of this whenever the need arises.

More Information

For more information on **the liver** see pages 49–51.

STEP BACK/REPULSE MONKEY

As you step back, sink into the heel of your standing leg. Keep your nose over your navel, but look just beyond your hands. Repeat the sequence at least nine times. When you have finished, store chi in the lower tan tien.

2 *While inhaling, sink on to the right leg as you lift the left leg and hand together.*

1 *Start with the left foot a step forwards, with the left hand down and the right hand up.*

Monkeying around
*Don't mimic a monkey,
just move naturally.*

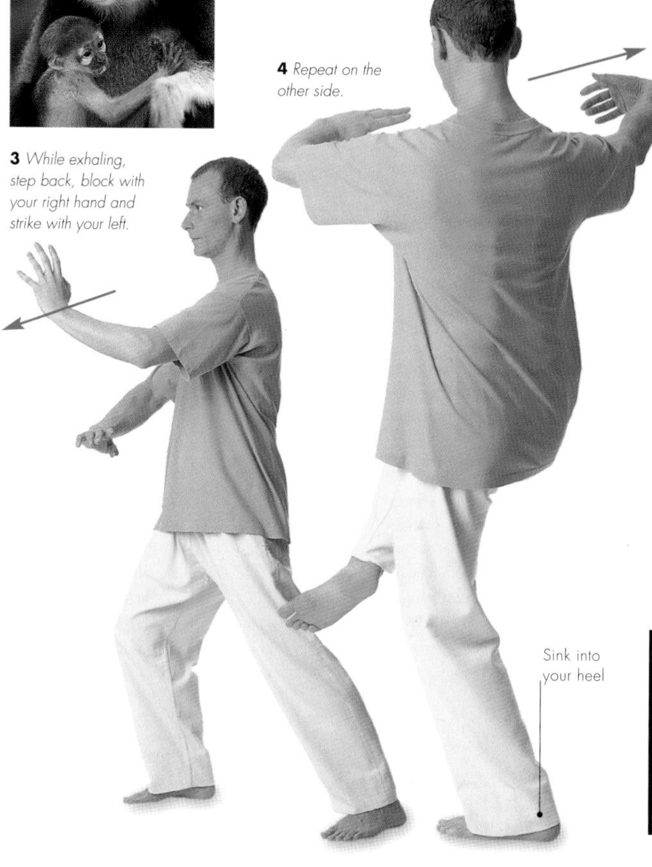

4 *Repeat on the
other side.*

3 *While exhaling,
step back, block with
your right hand and
strike with your left.*

Sink into
your heel

Sitting Like a Duck

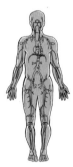

Circulation
This exercise boosts the circulation without putting a strain on the heart.

This sequence of chi kung movements will rejuvenate the whole body and invigorate the circulation. Beginners should practise the sequence slowly. The slow, continuous, smooth-flowing movement encourages the chi to flow in a very healing way. When you are comfortable with the movement, it can be practised a little faster, allowing the centrifugal and centripetal forces that are generated to invigorate the circulation to the extremities.

People with hip and knee problems should not practise this sequence since it may place too much pressure on these joints. Instead, here is a very gentle alternative exercise that will massage the internal organs and help circulation.

Standing in The Wu Chi Posture, turn your waist to the right and left, keeping the upper body relaxed and loose as you turn from side to side. It is very important to relax the shoulders. The arms are thrown outwards by the centrifugal force.

This exercise increases the circulation of blood and chi to the extremities without straining the heart, so boosting your health. The rotating and twisting massage all the internal organs, which are the reservoirs of the body's energy, so this exercise encourages chi and essence to flow from them through the entire meridian system.

More Information

For more information on **chi kung** see pages 220–221.

TSAN TUNG CHI

*Return to wu chi and
embrace your spirit.*

*Open and close as you turn
and the bones will grow firm.*

*The energy will move
like clouds and rain, limitless.*

WEI PO YANG

SITTING LIKE A DUCK
It is the vigorous rotation of the hips and belly, from side to side, which generates a rotational force that throws the arms out and back. There should be no tensing or contraction of the muscles in the shoulders.

2 *Turn the waist to the right.*

1 *Start with the weight on the right leg, the left foot a step forwards, with just the left toes on the ground. Hold the left hand down and the right hand up.*

Smooth moves

Your movements should be as smooth as water flowing off a duck's back.

Chin in

3 *Turn the waist to the left, and with the right arm going under the left, drop down to the floor. Sit back on your right heel with your arms crossed and the outside of the right knee on the ground, touching the left ankle. Hold for three minutes.*

4 *Rise straight up. Take a step forwards with the right foot, swap the arms, and repeat the move on the other side. Gather and store the chi in the lower tan tien after exercising.*

Sweeping the Lotus Root Kick

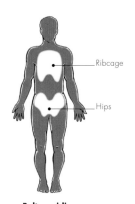

Ribcage

Hips

Belt meridian
This exercise activates the belt meridian connecting upper and lower body.

People suffering from bad circulation will be healed by this chi kung movement sequence. The power to perform the exercise comes from the torque generated by the counter-movement of the hips and the ribcage, twisting away from each other then back again. This twisting causes a compression and release on all the muscles, tendons, and organs in the body and creates a very invigorating rush of blood. Also, the thoracic diaphragm is massaged by the twisting movement. The centrifugal and centripetal forces generated by the waist rotation cause the chi to circulate from the belly to the extremities and back again.

The twisting of the body is also very good for activating the belt meridian, which runs around the waist and connects the upper body and lower body together as well as connecting the kidneys with the lower tan tien.

The power generated from the counter-torque of the ribs and hips is used a little in The Old Yang Style of Tai Chi, and much more in The 12 Qi Disruption Forms of Chang San Feng.

More Information

For more information on **Chang San Feng's tai chi** see pages 220–221.

TSAN TUNG CHI

*To try and gain health
without chi kung is like
hunting for rabbits underwater.*

Or looking for fish up a mountain.

*To make progress,
nourish your internal energy.*

WEI PO YANG

THE LOTUS ROOT KICK

This movement is from The Old Yang Style of Tai Chi, which is derived from The 12 Qi Disruption Forms. These are also the source of Pa Kua Chang, another internal martial art from mainland China, which uses counter-torque in almost every move.

1 *Start by positioning the feet in the shape of the letter T, with your hips turned to the left and your ribcage turned to the right.*

2 *Turn the waist to the right and the ribcage to the left as you slap the top of your right foot.*

Eyes look
beyond hand

Palms are
kept concave

3 Let the right foot land in front
and then repeat on the other side.
Gather and store the chi in the
lower tan tien after exercising.

Step Forwards to Seven Stars

This is a still chi kung posture, which is good for general health and for invigorating the circulation. There are two meanings to the seven stars description. The first alludes to the big dipper constellation (the one that looks like a frying pan). This is one of the star formations that can be a source of heavenly energy for chi kung. Secondly, when this posture is used for self-defence, the stars relate to what the opponent sees when he is hit.

This posture is held while balancing on one leg, with the knee bent. The exercise strengthens the standing leg, because it supports the body weight, and is also beneficial to balance. There are actually two types of balance – internal and external. To develop external balance, hold the front foot just off the ground. To develop internal balance, hold the front foot just off the ground and keep your eyes closed. The main aim of all chi kung, including tai chi, is to integrate internal and external balance and to harmonize mind, body, emotions, energy, and spirit.

Stand with one foot in front of the other. Place all the weight on the back leg and bend the knees. Hold the toes of the front foot just above the ground.

Shape the hands into relaxed fists and lift the arms in front of you, making a space under them. Although the hands are up, keep the shoulders relaxed and down, and, of course, relax the belly so that the chi can gather there and travel to the rest of the body.

Hold for three minutes on each side and repeat three times.

Gather and store the chi in the lower tan tien after exercising. This will keep you calm, steady and improve health.

More Information

For information on **storing chi** see pages 88–96.

Right hand
is yang

Left hand
is yin

Right hand
is yin

Left hand
is yang

All the
weight
is on the
rear heel

**Step Forwards
to Seven Stars**
*Both internal and
external balance can
be developed.*

THE SPIRIT BODY

The philosophy of chi kung is that we are more than just our physical bodies. Everybody has a spirit body that is a duplicate of the physical body, but is made of energy, not flesh. Instead of having veins with blood flowing through them, it has acupuncture meridians with chi flowing through them. Therefore, whenever we practise chi kung we are actually increasing our awareness of our spiritual body. It is even possible to leave the physical body temporarily and go travelling in the spirit body. It is understood that when the physical body finally stops working, it is possible to continue on one's journey in the spirit body. You do not change who you are, you will still be the same person you are now; however, there is much discussion as to where you go next – to wu chi, perhaps.

The Spirit Within the Body

The inner spirit
*Ancient texts liken the spirit body
to a baby in the womb.*

The first step on the path of spiritual development is to become aware of the spirit body within your physical body. We do this by imagining that a small duplicate of ourselves is sitting in the centre of our lower tan tien energy centre.

In many ancient texts, the development of the spirit body is described using the metaphor of a baby in the womb. By visualizing this for a few minutes every day, for at least nine months, you will nourish and protect your spirit body in preparation for other spiritual techniques. Our spirit body is made of chi. Every time you gather and store the chi in the lower tan tien energy centre after exercising, you consolidate your spirit and make it more substantial.

Getting to know the spirit

Right now you are inside your physical body, looking out of its eyes, and using its fingers to hold this book. We can use our spirit body in the same way, but we must be familiar with it. The processes of concentrating on and trying to develop the spirit body will result in your consciousness naturally being as comfortable in your spirit body as it is in your physical body. Eventually travel in our spirit bodies feels as natural as going for a walk. Many people, when they are asleep, report wonderful dreams of flying. Many of the chi kung techniques in this book cause the spirit body to become so full of chi that it expands beyond the confines of the physical body, sometimes expanding to fill the whole room. This is a great method of enhancing your awareness of your surroundings – it is like having an additional sense with which to interact with the environment. If you are training outdoors you can really feel as if you are not just existing amidst nature but are part of the earth and the trees.

The spirit body is accessible at the moment you are just about to fall asleep. You need to be familiar with this point for the next chi kung exercise, and able to recreate the moment between waking and sleeping. The exercise is practised sitting in a chair in a warm, quiet place with your feet on the ground and spine vertical and straight.

More Information

For information on **spirit travel** see pages 210–215.

Mind zest
Close your eyes and imagine squeezing a freshly cut lemon and smelling its sharp citrus tang. The power of the mind creates the experience of something that is not there. It is this same ability that we need to use to release our spirit body.

THE SPIRIT BODY ASCENDING

Imagine yourself in your spirit body, sitting in the centre of your own lower tan tien energy centre. To be born, the spirit body ascends the thrusting meridian and emerges from the top of the head, via the meridian point Governing 20 (G-20). As it does this you will feel an energy surge rushing up the thrusting meridian. At this moment, imagine a door of bright light opening, and the spirit body falling upwards through it.

Wide awake
We do not slip into unconsciousness – we maintain our conscious awareness as the spirit body ascends.

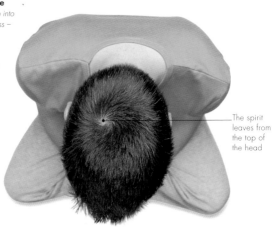

The spirit leaves from the top of the head

Beginners

Keep the spirit hovering just above your head and then return it to the belly.

The spirit is in
a cocoon of
protective energy

K-1 is rooted to the earth

Chi Kung for the Spirit Body

Journeying
*Not sleeping on earth,
but flying in the sky.*

Once you are comfortable with the experience of being outside yourself, you are able to proceed to the next stage. When you are outside yourself, on top of your own head, you should now practise all the exercises in this book again, but with your spirit body only.

This will have the double benefit of helping you develop a comfortable familiarity with having your consciousness in your spirit body rather than your physical body, and will also consolidate and strengthen your spirit body. It is important to remember to return the spirit body to the lower tan tien after each exercise.

The spirit body moves on

While you are alive, your spirit body is always connected to your physical body. To further the birth metaphor, one could say that there is an intangible umbilical cord of energy between the two. Metaphorically, physical death cuts this cord and you, in your spirit body, continue your journey.

If, while you are alive, you become familiar (through practising chi kung) with the process of being in your spirit body and leaving your physical body, the death of the physical body will be a smooth transition and you can concentrate on the journey ahead rather than becoming unsettled by the experience of swapping bodies. The transformation is a positive change, like a caterpillar becoming a butterfly and gaining the freedom of the skies.

Regular travel

Practise spiritual travel whilst in bed at night, where you are comfortable and will not be disturbed. As you are about to fall asleep, stay awake and fall up and out of the top of your head. Then turn around and look at your face, like looking in a mirror, but now you are the reflection. Don't use spiritual travel as a type of escapism from everyday life. It is best to get your mind, body, and emotions balanced before concentrating on the spiritual.

More Information

For more information on **spiritual matters** read and contemplate a wide variety of spiritual books.

SPIRITUAL TRAVELLING

It is up to you to decide how far you want to travel spiritually. I recommend small journeys first: go to the places you usually go to during the day. (Eventually you can choose to do and go where and when you want – for example you could go flying above the treetops in the countryside on a glorious sunny day.) The next step is to launch yourself straight into space. Fly past the moon, planets, sun, and stars, and absorb all their glowing energies into yourself. Then, while out in deep space, expand yourself until the whole universe fits inside you, and all the interacting yin–yang opposites that make up the universe are within you.

Journey into space
As you approach the point of going to sleep, fall up and out of your physical body and into your spirit body. Fly past the planets and into deep space.

The universe is within you

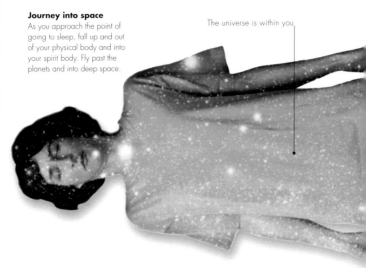

Transformation

Allow all the yin–yang opposites that make up the universe to enter inside you. Finally, go beyond yin and yang to become wu chi, the space that the universe is within, the empty circle.

Return to earth

When you return to your physical body in bed, and all you have is a vague memory of flying to the stars, you will wonder – was it real, or just a dream?

You are wu chi

GLOSSARY

Acupuncture meridian
An invisible energy
pathway in the body

**Acupuncture/meridian
point** A point of high
electric conductance,
where the energy in a
meridian can easily
be influenced

Bone breathing
"Breathing" (that is,
expanding and contracting
the chi) through any part
of the skeletal structure of
the body

Chakra One of seven
energy centres that is
located on the thrusting
meridian; associated with
Hindu yoga practitioners,
but also forms a part of
Buddhist teaching

Chang San Feng
Creator of the first style of
tai chi, which was known
as The 12 Chi Disruption
Forms, or Wu Dang
Mountain Tai Chi

Chi The animating life-
force energy within the
body; human "electricity"

Chi kung The literal
translation is energy work;
also used to refer to
breathing exercises

**Conception meridian
or vessel** The meridian
that runs up the front of the
body and which can
supply all the yin meridians

Daughter Posture A
standing posture similar to
the Mother Posture, which is
held for 15 minutes; it brings
chi through the elbows and
along the forearms

**Eight trigram paired
points** A group of eight
commonly used
acupuncture points

Father Posture A
standing posture similar to
the Mother Posture, which
is held for 15 minutes; it
brings chi through the
shoulder joints, upper back,
and neck

Five elements In
traditional Chinese
medicine the five elements
are wood, fire, earth,
metal, and water

Fu Xi Creator of the *I
Ching Book of Changes*

**Governing meridian
or vessel** The meridian
that runs up the back of
the body and which
can supply all the yang
meridians

Homeostasis The
process by which
opposing forces in the
body try to maintain
a balanced state as
environmental factors
around them change

***I Ching Book of
Changes*** The classic
Chinese book on the
workings of chi; it is known
in Chinese as *Yi Jing*

Kwa Literally "a
semicircular bridge", also
referred to as a bow;
there are two main kwa in
the body

Mother Posture A
still, standing posture that
is held for 15 minutes; it
releases chi from the lower
tan tien to the rest of
the body

Neuron A cell in the nervous system, which aids the flow of chi throughout the body

Pericardium The protective outer covering of the heart

Son Posture A standing posture similar to the Mother Posture, which is held for 15 minutes; it brings chi through the wrists into the hands

Spirit body A duplicate of the physical body, but consisting of energy rather than flesh

Spiritual travel Movement outside the physical body; most accessible just before you are about to fall asleep

Tai chi A martial art that heals the body, the mind, the emotions, and the spirit

Tan tien One of body's three energy centres, meaning literally "field of the elixir of life"; the centres are located just

below and behind the navel, behind the solar plexus, and between the eyebrows

Thrusting channel The meridian that runs up the centre of the body, and connects the three tan tien energy centres

Triple warmer As its name suggests, this comprises three warmers (the upper body cavity, middle body cavity, and lower body cavity), which help move heat around the body

Twelve organs In traditional Chinese medicine these are the lungs, spleen, heart, kidneys, pericardium, liver, large and small intestines, stomach, bladder, triple warmer, and gall bladder

Wu Chi Nothingness, the void, symbolized by an empty circle; also represents a spiritual dimension and a state of good health

Wu Chi Posture A standing posture similar to the Mother Posture, which is held for as long as necessary to receive whatever you need; it puts you into a state of receptivity to new ideas

Yang One aspect of the complementary opposites in Chinese philosophy; see also yin

Yang Lu Chan Creator of The Old Yang Style of Tai Chi

Yellow Emperor's Chinese Classic on Internal Medicine Another ancient Chinese book, which forms the basis of chi kung energy work; known in Chinese as Huang Di Nei Jing

Yin One aspect of the complementary opposites in Chinese philosophy; see also yang

Yin–yang harmony A state of equilibrium between the opposites of yin and yang

FURTHER READING

BRECHER, PAUL, *The Principles of Tai Chi*, Thorsons, UK, 1997

BRECHER, PAUL, *Tai Chi Directions*, Thorsons, UK, 2000

BRECHER, PAUL, *The Way of The Spiritual Warrior*, Godsfield Press, UK, 2000

CHANG AND CARRUTHERS, *Chen Pan Ling's Original Tai Chi Textbook*, Blitz, 1998

CHEN, *The Art of War*, Graham Brash, Singapore, 1988

Chinese Acupuncture and Moxibustion, Foreign Languages Press, China, 1987 and 1990

FLAWS, BOB, *Sticking to the Point, Volume 1: A Rational Methodology for the Step by Step Formulation and Administration of an Acupuncture Treatment*, Blue Poppy Press, UK, 1990

FLAWS, BOB, *The Dao of Increasing Longevity and Conserving One's Life*, Blue Poppy Press, UK, 1991

FLAWS, BOB, *Statements of Fact in Traditional Chinese Medicine*, Blue Poppy Press, UK, 1994

FLAWS, BOB, *70 Essential Traditional Chinese Medicine Formulas for Beginners*, Blue Poppy Press, UK, 1994

FLAWS, BOB, *The Secrets of Chinese Pulse Diagnosis*, second edition, Blue Poppy Press, UK, 1997

FLAWS, BOB, *Imperial Secrets of Health and Longevity*, Blue Poppy Press, UK, 1999

FLAWS, BOB, *630 Questions and Answers about Chinese Herbal Medicine: A Workbook and Study Guide*, Blue Poppy Press, UK, 1999

FLAWS, BOB AND DANIEL FINNEY, *A Compendium of Traditional Chinese Medicine Patterns and Treatments*, Blue Poppy Press, UK, 1996

FLAWS, BOB AND HONORA WOLF, *Prince Wen Hui's Cook: Chinese Dietary Therapy*, Paradigm, UK, 1985

FREKE, TIMOTHY AND PETER GANDY, *The Hermetica*, Piatkus, UK, 1997

LEFFMAN, DAVID, *The Rough Guide to China*, Rough Guides, UK, 2000

LU, HENRY, *Chinese System of Food Cures*, Sterling, USA, 1986

MONTAIGUE, ERLE, *Chinese Self Healing Methods*. Moontagu Books, Australia, 1999

MONTAIGUE, ERLE, *The Encyclopaedia of Dim-Mak and Acupuncture*, Paladin Press, USA, 1998

MONTAIGUE, ERLE AND ABIN, *Power Taijiquan*, Paladin Press, USA, 1996

OLSON, STUART, *The Jade Emperor's Mind Seal Classic*, Dragon Door, USA

THOMPSON, GEOFF, *Animal Day*, Summersdale, UK, 1995

WEYER, ROBERT, *Chuang Tzu in a Nutshell*, Hodder and Stoughton, UK, 1998

WONG, EVA, *The Pocket Tao Reader*, Shambhala, UK and USA, 1999

USEFUL ADDRESSES

Of all the people with whom I have studied over the last twenty years, there is one who is head and shoulders above the rest. Erle Montaigue, the leader of the World Tai Chi Boxing Association, is a man whose knowledge and ability in the internal martial arts and chi kung make him a living treasure. His international organization, the WTBA, has chi kung and tai chi instructors in over 40 countries.

To find a WTBA instructor near you, visit the website: www.taijiworld.com.

T'ai Chi and Qigong Centre Sydney
8 Beattie Street
Balmain
NSW 2041
Australia
Tel: (02) 9818 8229

For information about tai chi and chi kung in London please contact Paul Brecher, the London representative for the WTBA:

PO Box 13219
London
NW11 7WS
Tel: 020 8264 8074
Email: paul@taiji.net.

Paul also has free information about tai chi and chi kung on his website: www.taiji.net

INDEX